ORDAINED BY
ANGELS

A MEMOIR OF AN AIDS CHAPLAIN

by Father Jerry Anderson
with Shaun Sanders

SECOND EDITION

Manufactured in the United States of America
Cover Illustration, "Man of Sorrows", by Wesley Maxwell Lawton
Photography by Jim Shoemaker
Book design by Marc Borzelleca

ISBN-13: 978-0-578-40108-9

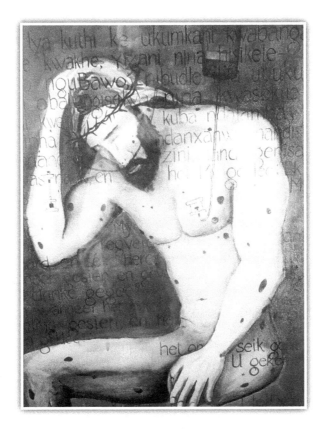

Dedicated To

Everett and Reva Reynolds Anderson
Thelma Imogene Anderson Harris
Shane Bruce

With great appreciation for
The Community Alliance Against AIDS
Miami, Florida

TESTIMONIALS

"In the fall of 1986 I was sent to a room at George Washington University Hospital to meet my newly assigned 'buddy.' I was a very untested volunteer with the Whitman-Walker Clinic assigned to be a supportive presence for someone living with AIDS. That is how I met Logan Sallada. And across his hospital bed that day I also met Father Jerry Anderson. Jerry, while a best friend of Logan's, also introduced himself as an AIDS Chaplain. What was an AIDS Chaplain? Jerry showed me. And he showed the seminarians at Wesley Theological Seminary how to live out the promise from Paul's Epistle to the Romans that nothing in all of creation will be able to separate us from the love of God."

The Reverend Dr. Chip Aldridge, Associate Dean for Admissions, Wesley Theological Seminary, Washington, D.C.

"With courage one seldom sees, Father Anderson stood in the front of the line with an attitude that 'you have to shoot me first.' When the darkness was overwhelming, he quietly held your hand. When no one else would touch you, he would anoint your head with oil. He embodied the courage that we needed so desperately to show that someone cared."

Matthew McGarvey, former board member of The Episcopal Caring Response to AIDS, Inc.

"God certainly blessed all of us who have had the Reverend Canon Jerry Anderson as part of our lives. And now through the words of his book, his readers will also be blessed. Jerry is a wonderful priest, a loving pastor and a caring human being. His work with HIV-AIDS, which began during the time most people were too scared to reach out to the individuals suffering from the disease, was filled with loving compassion that was a wonder to behold. Jerry brought peace and a touching love to those who many thought to be untouchable. I was privileged to make pastoral calls with Jerry, learning and developing pastoral skills which I have utilized for many years in my own ministry."

The Reverend N. Jean Rogers, an Episcopal Priest

"Jerry Anderson and his mission of creating The Episcopal Caring Response to AIDS (ECRA) in Washington, D.C. was a light of hope in what was a dark and troubled time for those with AIDS, their families and friends, and the church community. Jerry's leadership made it happen and gave strength to the weak-hearted and clarity to those confused about what the Christian response to the epidemic should be. He did all of this with grace and humor and a caring smile, attributes that come through in this personal story of his life and ministry with all of their challenges and successes."

Trevor Potter, Esquire, former legal counsel to
The Episcopal Caring Response To AIDS, Inc.

"I am sure Jerry knows exactly where his extraordinary courage comes from (a relative in Southern Illinois I am almost certain), but I have found it astonishing. To stand up again and again to power and power's institutions has always left me feeling a little weak-kneed. What an inspiration to all of us who lived in closets. Jerry would never tolerate those of us who could not bear another funeral as Jerry moved passionately further into the depths of the horror of HIV AIDS."

The Reverend Canon Skip Schueddig, Episcopal Priest

"I met the Rev. Jerry Anderson while I was on the run – from God, from the Church, from myself, from life. While taking mortgage application information from Jerry, I discovered that he was an Episcopal priest, out as a gay man, and Assistant Rector at a church in Washington, D.C. During an appointment I made with him very soon thereafter, Jerry invited me to "come home." He not only made that invitation, but he journeyed and prayed with me, mentored and encouraged me, as I worked to heal and make a home in a world and church that had persecuted me. Jerry's profound embodiment of God's transforming love saved and liberated me. That I am a happy and healthy lesbian woman and an Episcopal priest today is due in very large part to the extraordinary witness and ministry of Jerry Anderson."

The Rev. Susan Anderson-Smith

"A brilliant rendering of how a ministry of love and compassionate care helped individuals and families cope with the devastating effects of HIV / AIDS. This memoir is enlightening, uplifting and a must read for everyone who wants to connect with Spiritual power."

The Reverend Marilyn L. Hardy, M. Div D. Min.,
HIV/AIDS Prevention Educator

"Jerry's memoir is a must read for all who accompany others through pain, loss, death and grief. The story of The Rev. Jerry Anderson, an Episcopal priest, who stepped boldly into the unknown chaos of the AIDS epidemic and continued time and time again to hold in the presence of God people who were suffering and dying. As a father of two sons who in 1982 was taking in an orphan boy from Haiti with cancer, I was being told by doctors at NIH that if I did so, I would be risking the lives of my other boys. The supposed carriers of AIDS then were Haitians, IV users, and homosexuals. The times were filled with the fear of the unknown. Our world needed people with faith and courage. I needed such people. I then had the privilege of working with Jerry in our parish church in Washington DC and later of observing his work in Miami and Los Angeles. At every turn, I marveled at his way with all people. His fierce compassion was contagious. Jerry is a pioneer in the church and the world – a priest and a person who lives the Gospel -a priest and a person whose story is truly inspirational."

The Rev. Stephen R. Davenport III DD,
former Associate Rector of St. Patrick's Church.

"Jerry was so comfortable in his own gay skin as a priest, way before it became fashionable or easy to do so. I stood on the outside looking in for years as he served as Moses on the rock. Memories are short and I don't think that his true contribution or impact will ever be fully appreciated. But he was there, and I'm guessing, at times quite alone. I won't forget that or fail to honor it. I love him for the incredible man and priest that he is!"

Reverend John David Van Dooren

"Jerry's courage and tenacity to live a life of service in the church and the world (when neither really wanted him because he was openly gay) is remarkable. It is not only a story of hope and redemption, but it is a reminder how dreadful and destructive our self-righteous institutions can be. Where many gave up on organized religion, or were rejected by the church, Jerry and many like him became agents of reformation and redemption We live in a part of the Anglican Communion where LGBT people are welcomed, share their gifts in ministry, but this is still rare. Jerry's story is a reminder of the price some have had to pay so others can simply be respected as brothers and sisters in Christ today. His story is also a light in the distance for those who still struggle with ignorance and homophobia. Be the change you want to create. It works."

Reverend Albert Ogle, Episcopal Priest and
international advocate for gay rights.

"Jerry is one of the most gifted priests and pastors I have ever known. He served for me as a powerful role model in my "coming out process" and was a significant mentor as I journeyed toward ordained ministry. His vision and creation of the ministry "The Episcopal Caring Response to AIDS (ECRA)" in the Diocese of Washington, in a time of great oppression toward LBGT persons and particularly those with HIV/AIDS, touched countless lives and has made an indelible mark of love and compassion on all to whom he has ministered. Jerry is the true angel. His prayers, his healing presence, and his prophetic witness are gifts that I will always treasure."

The Rev. Dr. Joan E. Beilstein

CONTENTS

INTRODUCTION

This memoir has been thirty years in the writing. The title came to me one Sunday morning in church when I heard the story of young Stephen, the first Christian martyr, being read from the seventh chapter of the Book of the Acts of the Apostles. Stephen was preaching shortly before he was stoned to death, and he used the expression "ordained by angels." I instantly knew this had to be the title of my memoir. Why I reacted so strongly to Stephen's words has become much clearer as I have relived the many stories of my life and especially of my AIDS ministry.

One of the dictionary definitions of the word "ordained" is to invest with authority to act. What has become clear is that a host of persons throughout my life have contributed in clarifying my essential identity as a human being and a priest and in determining what my true destiny in life is all about. This includes friends who suffered with AIDS whose humanity deeply engaged my heart and soul, inevitably leading to a deeper and more profound understanding of how God's universe is interconnected.

There are many stories that I have not been able to include in this book, but they are also important as they touched and changed my life in profound ways. If I had written about all of them, this book would be much longer. My hope is that I have captured the essence of the spiritual transformation I experienced.

CHAPTER ONE

THE BIRTH OF AN EPIDEMIC

The summer of 1983 marked a watershed that would forever divide my life into two parts: before and after AIDS. I was 41 years old and living with my partner, Terry Parsons, in our townhouse on Capitol Hill in Washington, D.C. Up until then, I'd had the usual challenges of living in a country that viewed homosexuals as criminal, sinful and mentally ill. Those challenges paled by comparison with what was to come. That was the summer the AIDS epidemic hit home, gathering momentum as friends, loved ones, and strangers sickened and died within months.

Terry was working as an interior designer for the U.S Government, revamping office buildings all over the world, and I was happy with my career as an assistant rector at St. Patrick's Episcopal Church, just six miles from home. I'd come out as gay to my parish two years earlier and was helping to keep the parish on an even keel as we envisioned designing a beautiful new church building. Terry and I had an active social life, often hosting or attending dinner parties and taking part in various cultural activities. Our lives were flourishing.

The watershed arrived unexpectedly. Over the Fourth of July weekend that year, members of my family from Illinois and California were gathering for a big reunion in Fresno. Terry had no interest in attending the reunion, especially since most of my family members were either staunch Pentecostals or fervent Baptists. It was challenging enough that I was going—an Episcopal priest and gay into the bargain—but I was part of the family.

I flew into San Francisco, then rented a car and drove the 180 miles south to Fresno. Everyone was there: parents, sisters, my brother and his family, nephews and nieces, cousins, aunts and uncles. Altogether, there were more than sixty of us in two big houses and several RV's. Among my contemporaries, I was the only person not yet married. Some may have guessed I was still single at that age because I was gay. My immediate family knew, because I'd told them a decade earlier. Everyone else was too polite to mention it.

Although you could accurately describe my clan as fervently religious, they weren't tedious about it, and we were there to have fun. The time passed quickly, filled with story-telling, gospel-singing, fishing, horseshoes, and water skiing. My Uncle Booster even preached a sermon on Sunday. I was amazed by how much fun my Scots-Irish family could have without drugs or alcohol, pleasures that were de rigueur among my friends in Washington. I took occasional breaks to smoke pot on my own, but generally speaking we kept to good, clean fun. Unlike some pot smokers, I wasn't prone to paranoia, so that wasn't a problem. Any longer than four days and we might have started to get into the nitty-gritty, but that was just the right amount of time to enjoy each other and catch up on family news. My spirits were buoyed by our time together, and I was sorry to say goodbye.

I drove back up to San Francisco, but before flying home to D.C. I wanted to spend a few days with a longtime friend and mentor, Father Jack Harris. Like me, Jack was gay. I'd known him since my college days in Carbondale, Illinois where he had baptized me into the Episcopal Church. More recently he'd been hard at work rejuvenating Holy Innocents, a struggling church in the Mission District in San Francisco. I was looking forward to the visit, not only because I'd see Jack, but because I needed to let loose after being so well behaved at my family reunion. Jack knew how to have my kind of fun. I'd be able to have a drink and let my hair down. Little did I know that fun would be in short supply. I'd always had a great time in San Francisco, but this visit was to prove strikingly different.

Over dinner, Jack and two other friends poured out their hearts about friends of theirs coming down with terrifying symptoms followed by sudden death. Their stories filled me with dread. Developed countries hadn't seen anything like this since the discovery of antibiotics and vaccines, and I could scarcely believe my ears. Naturally, nobody wanted to party. Jack and his friends were depressed, and the mood was catching. I'd read one short article in Time magazine about gay men dying in New York City and Los Angeles of strange illnesses, but the disease hadn't touched the lives of anyone I knew until now.

Jack told me that his parish was in crisis because a gay man with AIDS had come forward to receive communion at the altar rail. Seeing this, the treasurer of the parish had resigned in protest. To allay fears of contagion, the parish agreed to set aside the centuries-old tradition of drinking from a common cup as a symbol of unity. From now on, the priest would dip the consecrated wafers in the wine and place them on the tongues of those kneeling to receive the sacrament. This practice later became widespread and led to problems with disintegrating wafers, which many found unsettling. Far more unsettling was that people were dying of a heretofore unknown disease, and others were terrified they might catch it too.

Two days later, as I flew home to Washington D.C. and Terry, I couldn't shake the feeling of gloom that had settled over me. I consoled myself with the thought that at least I could look forward to joining Terry and our friends at Rehoboth Beach. Four of us had rented a house for two weeks of partying, and they'd gone on ahead.

After landing at Washington's National Airport, I stopped by our townhouse to pack a suitcase before driving the three hours to Rehoboth. Once again, things didn't go as planned. I arrived around 11p.m., and everyone else had already eaten. They'd been drinking and were out on a large screened-in patio celebrating the end of a playful summer's day. I loved a good party and should have been in my element, but something inside me wouldn't let up. I was still in shock and couldn't shrug it off. I decided to delay talking about what I'd learned in San Francisco until everyone was sober in the morning.

Waiting until morning didn't help. They didn't want to hear it. I needed to talk with someone about the stories I'd heard from Jack and his friends, but I may as well have been talking to a brick wall. I was told to lighten up, not to worry about it, just have fun. "Here, have a drink," they said. They were dismissive. A few days earlier in San Francisco, I'd been the one wanting to party hearty when nobody else was in the mood. Now, the situation was reversed. This time, I was the party pooper. I knew this, but I also knew the issue was urgent enough that I had to tell them about it. If I cared for these people as deeply as I thought I did, I had no choice. We were all at risk, and they needed to know about the threat before it was too late.

My world had turned upside down after glimpsing the specter of death in San Francisco, but I was whistling Dixie for all the difference it made to Terry and our friends. San Francisco was a long way off, and there was too much fun to be had in the moment. In their defense, they'd been lazing on the beach for three days and understandably didn't want to come back to reality just yet. But I was hurt at being dismissed so cavalierly, and my hurt slowly turned to anger. I was furious that they were so willfully oblivious to the approaching danger. I was more than a little unhinged.

I took long walks on the beach and spent a lot of time by myself. One evening I returned to find everyone getting dressed up for the tea dance at the Blue Moon cocktail lounge. Terry and David, a friend of ours who was also a priest, were making a big fuss over their outfits, giggling with excitement about the night ahead. The Blue Moon was a gay bar, the place to see and be seen over cocktails after a day at the beach, and a big crowd was expected. I couldn't get into the spirit. Before Terry left, I tried one last time to get him to listen to me, but in vain. He was as dismissive as he had been earlier, and off he went. This wasn't the first time he'd lost patience with my serious side, but I'd never been the boy who cried "Wolf!" This was real.

I got in the car and left the party, driving on and on through the night to get past the rage that was building inside me. Finally, I checked into a motel. I wasn't angry enough to want to kill anyone, but I would certainly have disrupted the party atmosphere if I'd gone back to the beach house. I couldn't sleep. I just lay there alone in that cheap motel, a ball of burning fury. Halfway through the night, I checked out, drove back to where we were staying, and did not talk about my San Francisco experience with Terry or anyone else in our group of friends. Soon it was no longer necessary. The specter I'd only heard about in California emerged into full view at home.

In less than a month, a close friend was admitted to the Washington Hospital Center with harrowing symptoms. Bill had been a good-looking, fun-loving, 32-year-old gay man with the world at his feet. We'd done a lot of partying together, but Bill took things further than I would dream of taking them. To celebrate his 30th birthday, he'd gone out and had sex with fifteen different men. Clearly, he didn't understand the danger of such behavior. Few people did at that time.

When I visited Bill in the hospital, he was running a high fever, mumbling incoherently, and thrashing about in his bed. His mother and sister were there, and they were horrified. Bill died within the week.

From then on, Death marched inexorably through the ranks of our friends, families, and lovers, killing us indiscriminately one by one. I witnessed that march at close range for over eighteen years. This is my story.

CHAPTER TWO

ROOTS

This memoir is not my story alone. It's also the story of my family. I would not have made the choices I made nor become the man and the priest I am without their influence and guidance. This is the story of how a young man from a devout, conservative, working-class Pentecostal family in Southern Illinois became an openly gay Episcopal priest near the counsels of power in our nation's capital.

I've returned to my roots many times over the years to reconnect with family and friends and be nurtured by their friendship and love. St. Augustine wrote, "Our hearts are restless until they rest in Thee." My experience also has been that our hearts find their rest in those with whom we've felt God's presence most deeply. If we're lucky, we find such rest with our families.

It may seem the apple has fallen far from the tree, but it's fallen remarkably often into its shade. My family has always loved and supported me. Revisiting my roots has been far easier for me than for so many gay men estranged from their families because of their homosexuality. Having grown up thinking that I was the black sheep because of my sexual identity confusion, it took me a long time to realize just how much love there was for me in the family.

I am the son of a coal miner. I was born on March 25, 1942, and raised in a coal mining town that sprang up in the first decade of the 20th century when two farmers found coal just below the surface of their cornfields. Their discovery led to others, and soon coal was found almost everywhere in that area of Southern Illinois. My hometown was named Herrin after a German Baptist preacher who had settled in the area many years before that.

The history of Herrin is rife with tales of gangsters, feuds, and the Ku Klux Klan. Books have been written about it. My father had an old copy of *The Bloody Vendetta* on his shelf when I was growing up. Written in the late 1870s, it describes a deadly feud between Republicans and Democrats after the Civil War. Another book from my childhood, *Bloody Williamson: A Chapter in American Lawlessness*, accurately characterized itself as a "riveting chronicle of violence and crime in a Southern Illinois county."

My family, like most Herrinites, had a deep sense of the history of the place. Debates continue to the present day as to who did what to whom under circumstances lost to all but the oldest memories. Locals don't generally push matters too far. They don't want to pour fuel on the embers of an old fire.

As a boy, I would sit around and listen to men talk about the horrors of coal mining: who got hurt, who got killed, and how big were the explosions that maimed and killed. My dad's father had also worked in the coal mines, but he had a bad leg, so he worked "on top." This meant he worked in the business office, weighing coal and taking care of the payroll. Being on top was always better for obvious reasons. As part of his job, Grandpa would ride into town on payday in a horse-drawn wagon protected by armed guards to collect the money from the bank to pay the coal miners.

The miners sometimes sounded like veterans of a war zone as they recounted stories of injury and death down in the pits. They also talked about union concerns with safety and management and occasional plans for a workers' strike. Thanks to these stories, I learned from an early age how people dealt with serious life issues under pressure.

One of the great dangers of mining coal is the release of noxious gases called firedamp, which created major problems. Many mine explosions occur when a buildup of firedamp is accidentally ignited. There were two major coal mine explosions when I was young, in 1946 and in 1951. Over 100 men were killed in each explosion. One of the mines was in West Frankfurt, only ten miles from our home. We also had smaller mine explosions from time to time. An uncle on my father's side was killed in 1940 when the shaft in which he was working collapsed.

I personally knew a couple of people who were maimed in work-related accidents. My sister Norma Jean's husband operated a machine designed to replace the pick axe by cutting directly into the coal face. This was around 1975. The miners had been lobbying for a protective steel covering to be installed over the machine operator's cage, but it was not yet in place. When the roof caved in on him, it took three hours to dig him out. He needed multiple back surgeries and never worked in the mines again.

One of my nephews, who was a year younger than I, was badly injured in the 1980s. Jimmy Dean was riding a coal cart inside a mineshaft when the cart came to a stop. Further up the line, another coal cart had broken loose and came racing down the track straight into Jimmy's cart. There were no seat belts or other protective devices, so Jimmy was hurled into the metal bar in front of him, causing major injuries to his head and face. Like my brother-in-law, Jimmy was never able to work in the coal mines again.

Such events leave an indelible impression on those who witness them. Growing up, I constantly heard stories about how desperate people can be for work, and what they'll do to feed their families when conditions are terrible. Desperate men will go to extraordinary lengths to ensure their families' survival, even resorting to savagery. A vivid example was the infamous Herrin Massacre of 1922, which involved my mother's uncle, Levy Mann.

The trouble started when W.J. Lester, the owner of a local mine, failed to abide by his agreement to honor a nationwide strike by the United Mineworkers of America in June of 1922. When prices for coal increased during the strike, Lester hired non-union "scabs" brought in from Chicago. Enraged by the threatened loss of their jobs, a couple hundred union miners, after a day of gunfire, were able to take control of Lester's mine by force.

The angry local miners rounded up the strikebreakers and herded them toward the train station, supposedly to put them on a train out of town. Matters got out of hand when several strikebreakers were shot on the way to the train station. By now in a bit of a frenzy, the local mob brought ten remaining strikebreakers into Herrin. Along the way, they passed in front of my Grandma Anderson's house. Because my grandmother was a woman who was always praying, neighbors came flocking to her house because they felt safer there. My great aunt, Irene Luckey, had fled to the back pasture to secure my grandmother's horse. One of the men ran up to her and seized the rope from around the horse's neck. The mob used the rope to hang a man in Harrison's Woods, a block from my grandmother's house where we often played years later as kids

My mother's Uncle Levy Mann was one of the men who marched the strikebreakers into town. Eyewitnesses reported that the mob made the strikebreakers dig their own graves in the city cemetery and then shot them while local citizens stood around and watched. For years, nobody acknowledged where the bodies were buried.

The miners' actions were reprehensible but far from un-provoked. Their violent protest was symptomatic of the strains suffered by desperate workers across the country. Miners in particular worked under dangerous and unhealthy conditions for meager pay. A different kind of firedamp had accumulated in Herrin, one born of poverty and fear. The area was primed for an explosion. When it came, it was deadly. The union miners killed twenty-two of the strikebreakers and their guards. The town and county were left with a national reputation for violence that still resonated powerfully in my childhood years.

Following an investigation by local authorities, the men deemed responsible for the massacre were arrested and put on trial for murder. The town's sympathies lay with its own, how-ever, and the accused were acquitted in short order.
My great-uncle, Levy Mann, was among the acquitted. He didn't escape the consequences of his alleged actions altogether. Following the trial, he turned his back on his family without ex-planation. He would pass them in the streets and on their porches and never say a word. He became a recluse and a living reminder of our family's connection to the long-ago tragedy.

In recent times, a team of investigators led by an Illinois geolo-gist and historian discovered the location of the massacre victims' graves. They had been buried in potter's field in unmarked graves. Three or four of them were veterans of World War I, and one was a decorated soldier from the Great War. They were able to identify all the men, and a monument has been erected on the site, with all of the names listed, to honor their memories. It turns out that the man hanged with my grandmother's rope was Robert Anderson (not a relative).

It's been nearly a hundred years since the massacre took place, but the story of what happened and who was responsible still stirs up local debate. As a sensitive child, I found these stories gruesome. I knew from early on that I was not going to be a coal miner. I didn't have the courage or the temperament for dangerous work deep within the ground.

Local lore exerted a powerful influence during my formative years, but family tales and dramas made an even greater impression.

In the last summer before America's entry into World War II, Dad spent his days down in the coal mines, and Mom managed affairs above ground while pregnant with a third child. She was chief cook and bottle washer in a farmhouse packed to the rafters with extended family members: her widowed mother, her grandfather, an uncle, and her youngest sister, not to mention a husband and two children of her own.

Mom lost her third child in the summer of 1940. My brother, Ralph Waldo, died eight days after he was born. Within the family, there were two theories about Ralph's death. My father always said that the doctor in attendance had punctured Ralph's skull with forceps and caused bleeding in the brain. My older siblings were convinced Ralph died because mom's body was weakened by the grueling work of managing the household in the months leading up to his birth.

My mother didn't have great faith in doctors, but when she was about to give birth to me fifteen months after Ralph Waldo died, she decided to go to the hospital. My parents weren't taking any chances the next time around. As fate would have it, the doctor went home for dinner just before I arrived on the scene, so he wasn't there when I actually popped out. So much for doctors. Two years later, Mom stayed home and gave birth to my sister Norma Jean in January on a warm bed behind the coal stove. I was the only one of her children to be born in a hospital.

Altogether, there were five of us: James Everett Anderson, my eldest brother, born in 1923; my elder sister, Thelma Imogene, who came along in 1929; Ralph Waldo, who died in infancy in 1940; yours truly, in 1942; and finally, my younger sister, Norma Jean, born in 1944.

My mother, Reva Mae, was born in 1905 in a two-story
log house. She weighed 3 pounds, and to keep her warm they
wrapped her up in a blanket and set her in the oven. She was
called Reva Jack, on account of her tomboy tendencies. Mom
was a country girl through and through. One of ten children, she
never lived more than three miles from where she was born. She
was the spunky sister, a "can-do, will-do" type, and cooking was
her specialty. Reva was an Earth Mother before the phrase was
invented. Our house was the family's Grand Central Station, the
place where all our relatives gathered when they came to visit.

My mother was always cooking and having people over to
dinner. She cooked Southern soul food: collard greens, grits,
black eyed peas, cornbread, and fried chicken. Her pot roasts
were legendary. Neighbors would sometimes give us squirrel
or rabbit, and Mom served them fried. My brother James was
a good hunter, so he used to go out with his .22 rifle and shoot
supper. Some Herrinites ate possum, but my mother thought
possums were disgusting, so I was spared that dish.

Mom married my father when she was 18 years old. After
she joined the Pentecostals, she never again wore makeup or
earrings, and she never cut her hair. This proved advantageous
in the 1970s when the bouffant look came in style. Mom was
able to sweep up her hair in the latest style without breaking
any of the church's rules. Her side of the family remained mostly Baptists. Their slightly more relaxed approach helped balance
the rigidity of the Pentecostals on my father's side.

My father, Everett Ray Anderson, was born in 1901 in a small
town only four miles from Herrin. He was a smart man, like
his father before him. If he hadn't had to go to work in the coal
mines at the age of sixteen to support his family, he would probably have gone on to college to get a teacher's degree.

My father's nickname was Trap, a moniker given him as a
teenager when he worked in the coal mines as a "trapper." His
job was to open and close trap doors at regular intervals to keep
the mules that hauled the coal trucks up and down the shafts
from moving ahead of the work in progress. My mom called
him Trap throughout their married life.

My grandfather and my Dad's older brother died within a
year of each other, making it necessary for Dad to start working
in the coal mines to support the family. In Williamson County,

there were few options for work other than the coal mines for people without much education. The miners were at the mercy of the mining companies, with their regular lay-offs and down-times. During the 1940s when demand for coal was high, Dad worked double shifts, sixteen hours at a stretch. He eventually succumbed to tuberculosis after years of breaking up coal seams with a hand-held pickaxe and breathing in the dust while standing in pools of water. To escape the mines in his 50's, my father took courses at the vocational branch of Southern Illinois University and became a certified electrician. This was a great relief for all of us. For the last ten years of his working life, Dad was spared the dangers of working deep underground.

People liked and respected my father. Our pastor from those years, Brother Van Hoose, returned to Herrin for my father's funeral and eulogized him as "an iron fist in a velvet glove." This characterization aptly described Dad's gentle demeanor coupled with a steadfast determination in pursuing what he thought was right. He was a man of principle, and we always knew where he stood on any given issue.

Dad was not a hands-on father with his children. He believed in the maxim that if he gave us enough rope, we'd either hang ourselves or hoist ourselves to where we ought to be. Mom was the opposite. She was closely involved with all of us, to the point of being intrusive at times—exactly the way parents need to be with unruly children. I knew I could go just so far with mom, and then Dad would take over. He would never threaten us. A stern look was enough to do the job.

While my father "came from the head," my mother "came from the heart." She attended all of my events throughout grade school and high school. She was a stay-at-home mom, as was common then, and she had her hands full raising her family. She was a cheerleader for excellence and unflagging in her support for her children. When I tried my hand at art in junior high, she framed my best works and left them hanging on the walls of her home until the day she died.

My parents were happily married for 68 years. Even though they had only one income, they owned our house, and we never lacked for necessities. They were respected citizens and devout Christians. Theirs was known as "the best marriage" on my mother's side of the family. I was proud of that reputation, but it cast a long shadow, as I was to learn later on.

Dad "brought home the bacon," and Mom generally deferred to him, as was traditional in their community and church in those days. We all followed his lead on politics: We were staunch, pro-labor Roosevelt Democrats. My parents believed that Franklin Roosevelt's New Deal reforms had saved them and other working-class families from economic ruin.

My parents were deeply religious. They believed in following Jesus and did their best to honor his teachings in their daily lives. Many of our neighbors were poor and led hard lives that made them feel like hard people to a child. By contrast, our family unit felt like a bucolic island in the "sea of sinners" that made up the broader community. I saw Dad as gentleman among brutes. I later came to realize I'd judged the rest of our town unfairly, but I never lost my perception of my father as a Christian gentleman.

My parents joined the United Pentecostal Church in their 20's after Dad's mother, Myrtle Anderson, converted to the Pentecostal faith. They were married by that time, and my mother probably converted to keep her husband happy. I once teasingly asked my mother in her old age, "Mom, you're still really a Baptist, aren't you?" Her only response was a knowing smile. We both knew she was not the fiery, Pentecostal type. It was my father's side of the family that produced all the preachers.

Pentecostals believed theirs was the true religion and took care to distinguish themselves from the Baptists in any way they could. My Pentecostal father was worried about Grandma Reynolds' salvation. Although he loved his mother-in-law and thought she was a wonderful human being, she had died a Baptist. He then had a dream in which he saw Grandma Reynolds smiling and skipping across a body of water. He took this as a vision from Heaven: Grandma had been spared the fires of Hell and was rejoicing in Heaven. This boded well for the rest of my mother's side of the family.

Deferential and self-contained, Dad was a model deacon in our Pentecostal church. When I was growing up, he led the first half of the worship service and sometimes preached. He was always up-front in the sanctuary. Despite encouragement from many to become a pastor of his own congregation, he felt as if he was not charismatic enough to lead a congregation. For fifteen years he assisted Brother Van Hoose, the pastor with whom Dad literally helped build our Pentecostal church building. When Brother Van Hoose moved on to greener pastures in the larger city of Evansville, Indiana, he pressured my father to take over the running of the church that they had built together. Dad declined. He was happy to remain in a supporting role.

As Pentecostals, we were in church whenever the doors were open, often several times per week for regular services and every night during charismatic revivals. Revivals usually lasted for a minimum of two weeks. People fasted and prayed for days in preparation. The revivals usually took place in the church, but sometimes the evangelists would erect a big tent with sawdust on the ground to accommodate larger crowds. Revivals weren't circuses, but they did offer entertainment. People would publicly confess their sins, be slain in the spirit through the laying on of hands, and fall to the ground in ecstasy while speaking in tongues. There were no snakes, though. That was West Virginia, and we considered ourselves above that kind of thing. It was not uncommon for locals to sit in their cars on hot summer nights as spectators to listen to the music and preaching.

Dad had a large vegetable garden behind our house. I loved gardening and had my own plot for flowers for as far back as I can remember. Our neighbor, Mrs. Reynolds, was a kind and gentle soul who'd lived next door to us for decades. She taught me everything I know about growing flowers. I would shadow her in her own garden, watching and learning from everything she did. She gave me little plantings and taught me how to take cuttings from a rose bush, so they'd take root. Hers was a gift that kept on giving. We spent hours together, and I've been growing flowers ever since.

Up until about the age of 11, I preferred being with girls. I have a picture taken from when I was 8 years old of me sitting on a tractor with a bunch of other kids. We were all tucked in together, and I was the only boy among seven little girls. The tractor belonged to a neighbor, Coy Propes, whose daughter Judy was my best friend and a kissing cousin.

I spent a lot of time with these girls. We were a happy lot. We crocheted together, played dolls, and loved to get dressed up in women's clothes. One day Judy, her sister Donna, and my sister Norma, and I all got dressed up in hats and high heels and walked down the street together. We walked passed the house of Barney Woolard, another kissing cousin. It sometimes seemed I was related to half the people in our county. Barney was my age and was playing out in the front yard with some cousins from out of town. His aunt was out in the yard with them when she looked up at us and said, "Oh, look at those cute little girls."

Barney knew better. "One of them's not a girl!" he shouted. I shrank into my childish drag and looked away.

I played ball-and-jacks and jumped rope with the girls. As I got older, I realized that boys and girls were different, but I'd adopted the mannerisms of my girl friends. There's a revealing snapshot from that time of several of us kids sitting on the chromed front bumper of an old truck. I was there with my cousin Butch, my sister Norma, and my cousin Carolyn Sue. Butch looked like every other boy in a typical male pose with legs apart and arms crossed. I, however, sat there with my legs pressed together and my hands on my knees, just like the girls.

The moment I saw that photo, I knew it captured something fundamental about my nature. That would be obvious to anyone else who saw it, of course, and that wasn't to my advantage in 1950's Herrin, Illinois.

There's another photo from that era taken at my 14th birthday party. My extended family and I are gathered in the kitchen in a Rockwellian pose as I blow out the candles on my birthday cake. My stance and expression are stereotypically gay, even when viewed a half-century later. The rest of my family are looking on with affectionate indulgence.

In retrospect, it's remarkable that I managed to get by all those years without anyone trying to "butch me up." We often hear about boys like me whose fathers are determined to make them into "real men," and whose mothers criticize them out of fear. I never once heard that kind of criticism from the adults in my life. Despite the support of my family, my ventures out into the "real world" left me feeling insecure and inferior. I didn't "measure up" against the other boys as a typical male. I sensed a discontinuity between how I felt at home and how I was seen by the broader community.

Although my sensibilities were unlike those of other boys, I never thought of myself as gay. I'd never even heard of homosexuality. It was all about whether or not I was a sissy and whether I'd ever be able to fit in as one of the guys. That was a major concern as I became a teenager. I was awkward, uncoordinated and no good at sports. I was always the last to be picked for sports teams, and that left me feeling ashamed and embarrassed.

Because I didn't understand what it meant to be gay, I was unaware of any sort of gay community in Herrin. I did sense that a few of the older men were different from their peers. When I was 6 and my older sister, Thelma, was about 19, she dated one of the local "sissies," otherwise known as "fairies." His name was Parley Popham. In the 1950s, Parley was one of the Herrin men about whom it was said, "he swished." He wore tight clothes and was effeminate. Our pastor told Thelma she had to stop dating Parley because he'd left the church and taken to sin. He made it clear that if she didn't stop dating him, she'd have to stop singing in the choir. She loved the choir, so she quit seeing Parley. I did not want to end up like Parley when I grew up.

I didn't even want to end up as I was. Other boys liked to tease me. I was especially vulnerable when snakes were used as a prop. I was terrified of snakes, regardless of whether or not they were poisonous. I could become entertainingly hysterical at the sight of them. I'll never forget the afternoon I was playing with the girls, and Jerry Ditto and some older boys decided to chase me up a tree while waving a snake in my direction. They chased me across a field and up into an apple tree where I sat screaming at the top of my lungs. Fifteen years ago, Jerry Ditto came up to me at the graduation of one of my great-nephews and asked if I remembered the time he'd chased me with a snake. "I certainly do," I replied. Jerry apologized with genuine regret. I must have thrown quite a fit indeed for him to feel such regret nearly a half-century later.

Looking back on those times as an adult, I'm amazed that neither my mother nor my father ever said, "You can't dress up like a girl," or "You can't scream like a girl." They never said, "You can't go to the sewing circle. Boys don't crochet." Nobody in the family ever criticized me along those lines. They were extraordinarily accepting.

When I came out to my family in 1974 after much psychotherapy, my mother's greatest fear was that I would lose my job for being gay or that society would reject me. My mother wasn't educated and didn't read much, so she probably thought I'd been made gay rather than born gay. She must have had some confusion about that since she'd witnessed that I was different even as a child. In any event, she and my father were genuinely friendly to all of my boyfriends over the years. They came to visit Terry and me in our Washington, D.C. townhouse in the 1970s and were fully aware that we were lovers. When I think about how many gay teenagers in this country are homeless because their parents have rejected them, I'm reminded how lucky I was to have the parents I had. My mother and father exemplified the attributes of spiritually mature Christians. They not only believed in divine love, they practiced it toward others.

The only hard part about growing up as I did was that my father's emotional distance and the town of Herrin's limited sense of the world beyond the coal mines were psychologically and professionally isolating. I was never cut out to work in the mines, and I knew it. As soon as I reached the age of 18, I left Herrin for college and never looked back.

CHAPTER THREE

LEAVING HOME

As a teenager during the 1950s, I was riveted by news stories about the civil rights movement on television. The movie *Imitation of Life* made a profound impression on me. It's the story of a light-skinned black girl who was able to pass for white and did so, only later to realize she had betrayed and lost the most precious gifts in her life, her dark-skinned mother and her heritage. The struggle for racial integration was everywhere in the news. In 1957 there were violent protests against desegregation in Little Rock, Arkansas, a few hundred miles away from my hometown.

Little Rock's all-white Central High School became a battleground when nine black students were chosen to integrate the facility. Angry protests from the white community followed. Orval Faubus, the Governor of Arkansas, had state troopers surround the school to block the federal government's desegregation orders. Finally, Dwight Eisenhower, a fairly conservative Republican president, sent in federal troops to enforce the law. Scenes of white mobs jeering the black students filled the television screen and my mind.

With all the idealized passion of youth, I took up the debate on racial justice with anyone who felt otherwise. Later, when I became fully conscious of my homosexual orientation, I realized that my passion arose in part from a personal identification with the black community's challenges. I, too, was a minority.

Herrin was a "sundown town" in the 1950s. That was the term for all-white towns that enforced ordinances requiring blacks to be out of town by sundown. There were at least a thousand such towns across America in that era. African Americans needing to travel relied heavily on *The Negro Motorist Green Book*, a guide listing dangerous areas and safe havens along major routes. The mere existence of such a guide was damning evidence of the extent of racism in self-proclaimed Christian communities across the country.

The Walkers, an Episcopal family, had owned a men's clothing store in Herrin for several generations. Like other people of means, they hired black women as maids who would sometimes stay overnight. My friend Jon Walker recently told me that their maid would go around the house before it got dark and close all the blinds. She never answered the door after dusk. As a boy, he could never understand this behavior. Only later in life did he realize that she was hiding her presence in the town after sundown.

By the time I was 13 or so, I was old enough to get a haircut on my own and began to pay attention to the conversations around me in the barbershop. There were always several men hanging out there, airing their views with each other and the barber, Charlie. On one occasion, the topic was the recent decision by the school board to allow black students from two nearby coal mining towns to attend Herrin High School. This was a year before the 1954 Supreme Court ruling in Brown v. Board of Education.

As Charlie's clippers swirled around my head, so did the threats from other customers about what they were going to do. One of the men said to Charlie, "You know, you're gonna hafta cut their hair." Two other men recalled the number of "niggers" they'd killed in Alabama. In the middle of all this, Charlie was teasing me about how I must surely be "jacking off" now that I had pimples.

I felt utter revulsion that day in the barber's chair. I was mortified by Charlie's speculations. I had no idea whether pimples were caused by jacking off, but I'd heard you could go blind from masturbation, so why not get pimples? But it was the "how many niggers we killed in Alabama" talk that rooted me to the chair. I said nothing in reply. I was paralyzed with embarrassment, anger and fear. What could a teenage kid say to these murderous bigots? I might lose an ear or worse if I spoke up. This was my first direct experience of unfiltered racism, and I've never forgotten the impotence and complicity of my silence.

As I matured, I came to see that the Pentecostal church was not all it pretended to be. Our Pentecostal community was made up of close-knit families who were supportive and loving with each other but didn't always love other people. I sensed early on that there was an undercurrent of hypocrisy in the songs we sang and the sermons we heard preached. We'd sing the words, "Jesus loves the little children, all the children of the world, red and yellow, black and white, they are precious in His sight," in Sunday School and then were taught that the black race was a result of Noah's curse upon the descendants of his son, Ham, who had looked upon his nakedness. Ham's descendants supposedly went into Africa and became slaves as part of their punishment. In earlier years, this story from the book of Genesis had been used by Southern preachers to justify the "peculiar institution" of slavery in America.

There was a cruelty underlying Pentecostal church teachings that made a deep impression on children exposed to it. Hellfire-and-damnation sermons vividly portrayed the eternal torments awaiting those who failed to give their lives to Jesus. Sometimes I couldn't sleep at night for contemplating the agonies of the damned. What if I ended up among them?

I was baptized and "saved" at the age of 12. That didn't spare me from being scared stiff when I heard stories along the lines of "I saw Billy in church and the spirit was upon him to come to the Lord, but he resisted and then on the way home he was killed in an auto accident, and now he's damned in Hell forever." I heard many such cautionary tales designed to bring the faithful to heel through threats of retributive punishment, namely torture by fire.

There were quite a few things I didn't like about being Pentecostal. We couldn't go to movies, because they were a temptation to sin. We had to be conservative in our dress to avoid stimulating impure thoughts. We weren't allowed to dance for similar reasons. I resented such limitations deeply.

In 1958, my family and I drove down to Little Rock with other members of our church to attend the National Pentecostal Convention. I was determined to see Central High School where the historic integration drama had taken place the year before. After we arrived, I flashed my new driver's license and asked to have the car to drive over there by myself. The protests were over, and the campus was calm. The images from the year before were still lively in my mind though, and I was able to participate vicariously in that moment of history through the power of memory.

When I got back to the convention center, I learned that

the burning issue was whether or not Pentecostals could own television sets. There was no mention of school desegregation or racial equality – perhaps not surprising given that it was an all-white convention. After much debate, the Convention decided that Pentecostal preachers could not own TVs but that this rule shouldn't be enforced among the lay folk. They didn't want to foster divisive arguments possibly leading to divorce in families in which one of the adults might not be a "true believer" and insist on watching television while the other protested.

The deliberations about television reprised a debate held twenty years earlier on listening to radios. By the tender age of 16, I sensed there was something terribly wrong with these priorities. I began to rebel in high school. Although my parents had been strict with my older siblings, they eased their restrictions on movies and dancing with my younger sister and me. Even so, I found myself moving away from the church of my childhood as I looked forward to exploring the world beyond the city limits of Herrin.

I'm the only one of my siblings who went to college and the only one who ever expressed any interest in going. My parents knew nothing of college. I was ambitious, but my family offered only limited encouragement.

I was determined to attend the University of Illinois at Champaign-Urbana, a state university to the north of us. I had grand ideas about what I would do once I got there. I planned to major in political science, go to law school, then become a politician and do good works in the state legislature on behalf of the poor and the oppressed. That was my vision. I loved political science and American history. I idealized certain politicians and read everything I could about Abraham Lincoln. I subscribed to Time magazine when I was only 14 years old to keep informed on politics.

I got good grades in high school and was thrilled when I passed the university entrance exam. In the summer of 1960, my sister Thelma and my mother drove the 200 miles north with me to check out housing at my dream school in Central Illinois. This was a long drive before the interstate highway was built, and my mother was worried about what so great a distance might mean for our relationship and her ability to keep an eye on me.

I tried to reassure her by pointing out I'd be living in a Baptist boys' dorm, but to no avail. She wrung her hands all the way up and all the way back, moaning about how far away I'd be and how little money they had. Since I had no car, they'd have to drive 400 arduous, costly miles roundtrip any time they wanted to see me.

Despite my best efforts to convince Mom that everything would work out just fine, she wore me down. I finally gave in and applied instead to Southern Illinois University in Carbondale, just fifteen miles away from Herrin. That was to be my home for the next five years—except for one year when I was sidetracked by an ill-fated interlude at a Texas Bible college.

CHAPTER FOUR

Southern Illinois University

Every two weeks for the next year, my mother drove over to Carbondale with Aunt Clara or my nephew Jack to collect my dirty laundry, take it home, wash it, starch it, iron it, and bring it back. She pretended this was all about laundry, but the real reason for her visits was to make sure I wasn't getting myself into trouble.

Happily, I discovered that two weeks between maternal inspections gave me sufficient wriggle room. On arrival in Carbondale, I moved in with Tom Williams, a friend from high school who knew how to have fun and quickly taught me how to drink and smoke. Tom got me drunk the first week we were there and showed me the proper way to inhale tobacco smoke and blow it out through my nose. We were quite the young sophisticates.

Southern Illinois University was a large school with 20,000 students from all over the world. Although close to home in miles, it was worlds away in spirit. I felt liberated and challenged there. I joined the debate team the first year and considered pledging a fraternity. I wanted to prove that I could overcome my humble background and make it in a far more worldly environment. You can take the boy out of the country, but can you take the country out of the boy? I was determined to succeed.

For the first time, I claimed my constitutional right to freedom of religion. I began to explore other churches. I settled quickly on the Presbyterian Church, partly because it was so different from the Pentecostal Church. Services followed the order outlined in a weekly bulletin, and the minister gave well-organized, thought-provoking sermons. The choir was vested in colorful robes and sang beautiful music well. This was a far cry from my church in Herrin where sermons were judged more for their passion than their content and the style of worship varied with the mood of the congregation as the Holy Spirit moved among its members.

It does the Pentecostal preachers no disrespect to say that they were generally not well educated; they themselves took a stubborn pride in the fact. I was fortunate my parents allowed me to attend college at all. Many Pentecostals were convinced that godless, atheistic universities could damn the souls of unwary students for all eternity.

I relished getting away from all that, but my past was about to catch up with me in no uncertain terms. I spent one year at Southern Illinois University before the winds of change blew through my life—an intervening tempest masterminded by my Aunt Mary Letta.

CHAPTER FIVE

BIBLE COLLEGE

The "winds" picked up soon after I arrived home the summer after my first year of college. I'd been asked by my cousin Tom to be best man at his wedding up in Central Illinois. Tom was two years older, handsome and athletic, and I idolized him. He'd just graduated from the International Bible College in San Antonio, Texas and was marrying a woman who'd also graduated from there. Their wedding took place on an extremely hot July afternoon with temps reaching 105 degrees in the shade. There was no air conditioning in the little Pentecostal church where the wedding took place, and it got so hot that the candles started melting to the side. When they leaned so far over that they were burning into themselves, the ushers had to put them out.

Stepping up the heat was Aunt Mary Letta who'd flown out from California for the wedding. Aunt Mary Letta was the wife of my father's youngest brother, Uncle Booster, who pastored a Pentecostal Church in Oakdale, California. She was a righteous, conservative, matriarchal force to be reckoned with. Bright and articulate, she was a robust woman with a ruddy complexion, reddish-blonde hair, and horn-rimmed spectacles. Despite the Pentecostal law against it, she kept her hair on the short side but conformed by wearing no makeup.

Immediately after my cousin's wedding, Mary Letta returned with us to Herrin and stayed for a few days. It took her less than an hour to turn her keenly perceptive gaze on me. What was I doing with my life? Was I on the right path? She sensed that I had strayed from the straight and narrow.

A year of college hadn't completely drained the Puritan ethic from my conscience, and I did feel some guilt about drinking and smoking and trying out other churches. Aunt Mary Letta wasted no time before laying the "fear of the Holy Spirit" on me. She'd heard I was attending a Presbyterian church and falling away from the true faith. I was, she proclaimed, a "backslider." Mary Letta had a powerful personality, and I fell all too easily under her spell. That same evening, I drove over to a prayer meeting at the First Apostolic Church where I'd grown up, fell to my knees, confessed my sins, and asked God to come back into my life. The next morning, I announced to great rejoicing that instead of returning to Southern Illinois University, I was going to go to my cousin Tom's Bible college.

In hindsight, it's clear that Aunt Mary Letta did quite a number on me. That kind of pressure was not at all uncommon among Pentecostals. The older people took it as their duty to rain down hellfire and brimstone on young folks just to keep them on track. Today we'd call it guilt-tripping.

My decision to reform my life happened the first week of August, and the fall semester wasn't far off. I stopped smoking, I stopped drinking, and six weeks later, my parents drove me to St. Louis and put me on a train to San Antonio. I was excited about taking the train to Texas. I'd never been there before, so this was an adventure.

On a Saturday afternoon, I boarded a train full of college students who were heading off to start their fall semester at the University of Texas. I hit it off with a few of them, and we got to partying, and that's when I tried tequila for the first time. I got drunk and passed out on the floor of the club car. When I woke up the next morning, it was dusty and hot, and the windows were open. We were in Texas, and I was hung over. I sat and waited, my head throbbing, for San Antonio to come into view.

I arrived on Sunday afternoon. I felt terrible and smelled like a brewery. There were two students from the Bible school waiting for me at the train station. They wore black suits and little black ties—this was in 1961—and they carried big Bibles under their arms. I don't remember what I was wearing, but it certainly wasn't a suit. I'd been on the train for 24 hours and hadn't showered. They were about my age, and one was from my Pentecostal church back in Herrin. Who knows what they were thinking. We got in the car, and they drove me up to the International Bible College. We didn't say much along the way.

The Bible college, run by Pentecostals, was situated on Hallelujah Hill on the outskirts of suburban San Antonio. I'd never even seen photos of the school, so I viewed it for the first time as we reached the top of the hill. Disappointment doesn't begin to describe my reaction. The campus was tacky beyond description. Any joy had been sucked out of the place long before my arrival.

International Bible College was founded during the Second World War by a missionary who'd been expelled from Japan. It consisted of army barracks that had been built elsewhere for other reasons and moved onto the site. You never saw anything so dreary in your life. The chapel, located in one of the barracks, made one think of anything but God. It was depressing as Hell just to be there. I knew I'd made a bad mistake.

At six o'clock that evening, we all headed down to San Antonio's main drag to conduct a street revival. Compared to Herrin, San Antonio was a bustling, exotic city. I hadn't even unpacked, and there we were with a bass drum and tambourines and a megaphone to catch the attention of the men and women on the street. We positioned ourselves next to a Catholic church, so we could grab the Catholics when they came out and tell them the truth about Jesus. We did that for an hour or so, then by 7:30 p.m. we'd moved on to Revival Temple, the church affiliated with the Bible college, for the Sunday night worship service.

I wanted to die. Only once or twice in my life have I realized early on that I'd made a terrible decision. This was one of those times. "What on earth have you done?" I thought.

Salvation appeared in the form of Scooter Radcliff. I was 19, and Scooter was 21. Scooter was also from a Pentecostal family and had undergone a conversion experience similar to mine when he returned home to Louisiana from New York University that summer. He, too, had rededicated his life to Christ and now found himself at the Bible college wondering what the hell he was doing there.

Scooter was always sneaking around smoking forbidden cigarettes, and it wasn't long before I joined him. It was during one of our smoking sessions that Scooter revealed he was gay and told me all about gay life. I was shocked. Then, when he informed me that the handsome, blonde movie icon Tab Hunter was gay, I was inspired. I had quite a crush on Tab Hunter and learning he was gay helped me begin accepting my own homosexuality.

One night during our second week in San Antonio, we told the dean of men that Scooter's parents were in town and that they were taking us out to dinner. We explained that we might be a little late, and that if we weren't back by curfew, it couldn't be helped. At least we'd be with God-fearing people. Which was mostly true. Except that it wasn't Scooter's parents who were in town; it was two cute friends who'd come down from Shreveport.

The three of them took me to a gay bar and got me drunk. We then headed over to the St. Mark's Hotel coffee shop to sober up, smoking cigarettes the whole time. I had to step outside and throw up at one point. I was prone to throwing up whenever I drank and smoked too much. I was wearing a necktie that night and threw up all over it, so I had to throw it away. I soon began to feel better, which was fortunate because I had sex with one of Scooter's friends in the back seat of the car at four o'clock in the morning. We got back to campus at five and had to get up at six in time for a shower and breakfast before chapel. Those first two weeks of Bible college gave me an impressive education.

That evening, Scooter took me aside and suggested we sneak out for more fun. My mind was still reeling from the night before, so I declined. My world had been turned upside down since the day I'd set foot on campus. Scooter had come out to me, told me about gay movie stars, and taken me to a gay bar. I'd been seduced by his cute friend. And I loved it—all of it.

As fate would have it, Scooter went without me. He snuck out and got caught, and they expelled him from Bible college. He had to pack up and leave immediately.

Brother Coote, the President of the college, told me that they'd almost kicked me out, too. I was spared by their fear that I'd go back to "that godless university" in Southern Illinois and lose my soul. That got my attention. The Pentecostal church back home had raised the money to send me off to Bible college, and members of the congregation had prophesied I was going to become a great preacher. I'd made a big public announcement of coming back to Jesus. I shuddered to think about the embarrassment my family would endure if I were to quit or be thrown out of the school.

I stayed at International Bible College for an entire year, most of which I spent trying to figure out how to escape it. I was bereft after Scooter left. He'd introduced me to another world, which I found exciting, and then abandoned me by getting kicked out. It was a deeply unsettling experience.

Once again, I was saved from despair, this time by my roommate, Worthy Rowe. Worthy and I had a lot in common. Like me, he was third generation Pentecostal. His grandfather had founded a Pentecostal church in Indiana, and his father was pastor of the church. Worthy had come to International Bible College to "test his vocation" and soon discovered he didn't have one. He was a clown and a cut-up and an all 'round delightful human being.

Thank God, he turned up when he did. He probably suspected something had gone on between me and Scooter, but we never talked about it. Worthy had a wicked sense of humor and enjoyed a good time. He loved girls and drove a Volkswagen Beetle convertible, which was pretty hip for the time. After curfew, we would push his Beetle slowly down the gravel drive at Hallelujah Hill, leap in as it built up speed, pop the clutch once we were out of earshot, and off we'd be on our way into town. Worthy had the timing down pat. On the return trip, he'd build up enough momentum so that he could kill the engine just at the right moment and still make it up to the parking lot without any noise giving us away.

Despite our occasional revels, most of the time we stuck with the program. We'd be up 6 a.m. for breakfast, then head straight over to chapel for services. There, if the spirit hit, people would start speaking in tongues. They might even be "slain in the Spirit," overwhelmed by spiritual ecstasy to the point of collapse. This was a bit much at that hour of the morning, and I always welcomed Worthy's comic relief. He could even roll his eyes without anybody hearing them.

Something else that helped me stay sane was my part-time job at the San Antonio Public Library. It was fairly menial work, but the library was in a lovely old building and offered a welcome respite from the Bible college. I found a spot where I could sit alone and look out over the desert sagebrush; it was my own sacred hideaway. I'd contemplate the view and have a good cry from time to time, wondering what on earth was going on with me. After all, I was only 19 years old and away from home for the first time.

And then a miracle happened. In 1962, after I'd been in the Bible college for a year that felt like eternity, Aunt Mary Letta and Uncle Booster invited me to spend the summer with them and study for the ministry under Uncle Booster in Oakdale, California. In normal times, I'd not have been keen on the idea, but these were not normal times. I wanted to get out of that school as quickly as possible, so much so that the thought of living with my Pentecostal relatives seemed like a step up. Too, I'd heard that my uncle had loosened some of the stricter Pentecostal rules in his household.

Alas, I discovered that once again I'd leapt from the frying pan into the fire. After I'd been in Oakdale for a couple of months, Booster—who was trying to groom me in his own image—learned I'd been out on an innocent date with a girl from the Episcopal Church. Booster turned out not to be as reformed as I'd been led to think. He became angry and lectured me in no uncertain terms that dating someone from outside the "true faith" was a serious violation of his rules.

This came as a surprise since my uncle had earlier given me permission to attend an 8 a.m. service at a local Episcopal church that was part of the charismatic renewal movement then sweeping through many mainline denominations. That was my first visit to an Episcopal Church, and the one service was all I needed to get hooked. I would go over to the church during my lunch hour from the Western Auto store where I was clerking that summer and sit and pray. The Presbyterians had paved the way, and this was the home to which the path led me.

I'd continued to struggle with my sexual orientation and had kept it hidden after Scooter was kicked out of the Bible college. Uncle Booster's attitude didn't encourage authenticity on my part. I cried myself to sleep the night after his angry lecture and the next day announced I was moving back to Herrin at the end of the summer. Once more, I set my sights on Southern Illinois University.

CHAPTER SIX

Return to Southern Illinois University

After escaping Uncle Booster and Aunt Mary Letta, I wasted no time getting back to civilization and renewing my studies at Southern Illinois University in Carbondale that fall. Within two weeks, I'd knocked on the rectory door of the local Episcopal church, St. Andrew's, and introduced myself to the rector, Father Jack Harris. I joined his confirmation class right away and began taking instruction in the faith. The church was conveniently located right next to the campus, and it hosted a gathering for students, the Canterbury Club, which I joined. The parish rented out rooms in a boys' dorm that housed sixteen students, and by January I'd secured a room there.

My mother wasn't happy about my drawing closer to the Episcopal Church, but I knew there was no turning back. In a matter of months, I announced to my family that I was going to be baptized—for a second time. The Pentecostal sect to which my family belonged baptized in the name of Jesus only. The Episcopal Church does not consider baptism to be authentic unless it's done in the name of the Trinity—the Father, the Son and the Holy Ghost.

Father Harris baptized me on Holy Saturday, Easter Eve of 1963. I can still hear his voice: "If thou art not already baptized, I baptize thee in the name of the Father, and of the Son, and the Holy Ghost." By that time, Father Harris and I had discussed my going on to seminary after college to study for the priesthood, so he took particular care to ensure that my baptism was valid using the trinitarian formula.

I was pleased that my mother and my older sister, Thelma, came to my baptism, even though I knew Mom mostly just wanted to see for herself what was going on in her son's life. My father joined my mother in attending my confirmation by the bishop several months later. I felt supported by their presence even though I later got the third degree from members of their Pentecostal church in Herrin who asked, entirely seriously, "How can you do this to your father?"

Joining the Episcopal Church was a liberating experience. One could occasionally curse as an Episcopalian without fear that the ground would open up and swallow you whole. Like anyone who has lived with spiritual oppression for a long time, I was thrilled to discover that it's possible to love God without scrupulosity or the feeling of being constantly judged and found wanting. I'd spent years around unctuous preachers who couldn't say "shit" if their mouths were full of it. They reminded me of the servant Joseph in Emily Bronte's *Wuthering Heights* in their ability to ransack the Bible, raking its promises to themselves while hurling its curses at their neighbors.

There was no prohibition on drinking alcohol in the Episcopal Church, a freedom I readily embraced. At the reception following my confirmation, Bishop Chambers told me with a wink, "If you're going to be an Episcopalian, you need to learn two things: how to play bridge, and how to make the perfect martini."

Wonder of wonders, I discovered there were gay members of St. Andrew's parish including Father Harris and the college chaplain, Father Fred Norman. Both priests were still in the closet, of course. In the 1960's, nobody in the church was out. Nevertheless, both were bachelors in their late 30's, and their homosexuality was an open secret in the gay community. My boxes were checked. I could hope to be myself and still be part of the life and worship of the church, even if I couldn't be entirely open about it.

College life once more proved challenging and fun. Immediately upon my return to Southern Illinois University, I joined a theatrical group that was part of the Southern Baptist student association. They were progressive for Baptists, going so far as to begin rehearsals for a performance of *Inherit the Wind*, a fictionalized account of the infamous 1925 Scopes "Monkey" Trial. I was cast as the Scopes character on trial for teaching evolution in defiance of state law. Two weeks into rehearsal, however, thirteen Baptist ministers from around the area signed a letter saying that if the director didn't stop production of the play, they would withdraw all financial support. Sadly, work on the play was halted. We went on to stage another play titled Christ in the Concrete City. It was so well received that we took it on tour along with the Baptist student choir.

I'd made progress in finding myself by returning to college and joining the Episcopal Church, but I was still a mixed-up and conflicted young man. One didn't come to terms with homosexuality easily in an era when to be gay was to be among the most despised of human beings. We were considered criminals under the law, sinners in the eyes of the church, and mentally ill by the psychiatric establishment. Many of us carried tremendous guilt. The consequences of acting on my true feelings could have been disastrous. That was confirmed by a traumatizing development close to home. Within a year of baptizing me, Father Harris was forced to resign after thirteen years as rector of St. Andrew's because he was found out as gay.

In those years, all young men grew up under the expectation that they would someday marry and have children. There was no other model. I dated girls, but there was little passion. What I did have were secretive affairs with other guys during my college years.

Father Norman, our university chaplain, became my rock, and I grew to adore him. He could offer earthy, pragmatic advice on any topic, and this helped me stay grounded. One day, feeling desperate, I told him, "I've got to have sex with a woman. I just can't do this anymore! I need to get straight." His laconic reply: "Jerry, there ain't no magic in pussy juice."

Once in his office, while berating myself, I swore "I'm never going to have sex with a man again, may God strike me dead!" Father Norman's response was, "Look, Jerry, human nature being what it is, you shouldn't make such absolute promises. If you fail again, you're only going to beat yourself up more severely." His words were both loving and wise, and they helped. He saved me from a pit of self-loathing.

I gradually came to accept myself more fully and soon met a small group of other gay students with whom I began to socialize. There were three seminarians in my new circle of friends. Bill and Jim had been two years ahead of me at Herrin High School, and Frank had grown up in a nearby town. All three were in different seminaries, and we soon discovered we were all gay. Bill had a Ford Fairlane convertible, and the four of us spent endless hours driving all over the state together in the summer of 1964.

One hot August night, we were parked out front of the Flamingo Lounge, the only gay bar in Carbondale, daring each other to go in. We knew that once we entered the bar, it would be understood by those inside that we, too, were gay. For at least a little while, in that time and in that place, we'd be out of our closets and no longer hiding.

When we finally mustered the courage to go in, we discovered the bar was illuminated by pink lights and almost empty. Most students were out of town for the summer. There were only four or five guys inside, and they were standing around a small grand piano singing show tunes with the piano player. As soon as we joined them at the piano, who should appear but Parley Popham, the flamboyant character from my hometown who'd dated my sister Thelma for a time.

Parley took one look at me and sailed across the dance floor screaming, "I told your sister when you were 6 years old you were going to be gay!" Parley was one of the reigning queens of Southern Illinois until the end of his life. He was a hoot. Gay friends of mine who attended his funeral years later reported that the Pentecostal preacher claimed Parley had repented of his sins before he died and was going to Heaven. I'm sure this wasn't the first time such fictions were reported in funeral eulogies. Such repentance would have required Parley to declare he was no longer gay, something no one who knew him could imagine he'd ever do.

We thought we were keeping a low profile that halcyon summer, but no such luck. Frank and Bill, both Roman Catholic, returned to their respective seminaries to find the doors barred against them. Both had been expelled. We'd attracted more notice than we'd realized. My Catholic friends were fairly sure that a particular Roman Catholic priest they knew had reported them to their bishop. Although they went on to other professions, our other seminarian friend, Jim, was eventually ordained as an Episcopal priest.

My final year of college was marvelous. My grades suffered somewhat because of my absorption in extra-curricular activities, but I managed not to disgrace myself. I did well in the subjects I liked: constitutional law, history, and psychology. I did less well in my language courses. At the end of the day, I graduated from Southern Illinois with a Bachelor of Arts degree in Liberal Arts.

CHAPTER SEVEN

New York City

My dream of becoming a lawyer lasted until I was 21 years old. It wasn't so much that I loved the idea of lawyering as that growing up in Herrin limited my perspective. I didn't realize I had other options besides the coal mines, the Pentecostal church or the law. I wasn't about to spend my life in the mines and couldn't imagine submitting to the austerities required of a Pentecostal preacher.

Becoming an Episcopalian broadened my horizons considerably. I'd always been drawn to the spiritual life but never felt entirely at home in the church in which I'd been raised. As I came to know and love the Episcopal Church, I found myself drawn to its ministry. By the time I graduated from Southern Illinois, I'd made up my mind: I wanted to become an Episcopal priest.

The Episcopal Church requires prospective ministers to run a gauntlet of examinations before they can be admitted to seminary. I had to be recommended by my local parish and approved by the Standing Committee of the Diocese of Springfield and accepted by the bishop. This involved extensive interviews and a thorough psychological assessment to weed out unacceptable candidates.

I was anxious, because I knew homosexuality was high on the list of disqualifications. I didn't know their exact formula for discerning whether someone was gay, but I knew they sometimes figured it out. After a series of interviews with lay and clerical leaders in the diocese, I met with the church's examining psychologist. After a probing conversation, she gave me a Rorschach test. I left without a clue as to how I'd done.

Later, on pins and needles, I sought out Father Norman to ask if he'd heard anything about my application. "You didn't raise any red flags," he assured me. "Don't worry about it."

I had somehow passed muster. Soon afterwards, I was invited to meet with the bishop who formally admitted me a Postulant for Holy Orders. I was accepted by the General Theological Seminary for its three-year program, and off I went to begin my studies in New York City.

Others weren't so lucky. I'm convinced that one of the three applicants from our diocese was eliminated because he was gay. After I entered seminary in New York, I met guys who'd been expelled from other seminaries for homosexuality. My seminary was slightly more progressive, but I was walking a tightrope. The fall was a long way down.

There were, of course, many gay clergymen serving in the Episcopal Church in those years. Quite a few of them led double lives, hiding their homosexuality behind a traditional heterosexual marriage. I had fantasies myself of marrying someday and keeping the truth about myself under wraps. Ironically, after Father Harris was ousted from St. Andrews, the married priest with seven children who took his place was also gay and closeted. Such marriages were usually unhappy for everyone concerned. Over time, many of them ended in divorce, and the husbands would find themselves back where they started. Some continued to live closeted lives; others would come out into the gay community.

The General Theological Seminary was located in the Chelsea neighborhood of Manhattan. It was founded in 1817 at St. Paul's Chapel in lower Manhattan but soon moved to the country estate of Clement Clarke Moore, best known as the author of 'Twas the Night before Christmas. By the time I entered as a student, its classrooms, faculty quarters and student dormitories enclosed an entire city block to create an interior quadrangle or "close" similar to that of many English universities.

The dorms took up four floors. Separated by corridors, the suites on either side had two bedrooms and a lounge. I shared a suite for the first year and was fortunate to have a private room for the following two years. There was a beautiful chapel in the center of the campus. We wore black academic gowns to class lectures and chapel services and met with tutors each week to discuss papers we'd written to their specifications. All things considered, the ambiance was far superior to my surroundings at the San Antonio International Bible College.

Our academic routine followed predictable rhythms. We had chapel first thing each morning and then breakfast afterwards. Classes began at 9 a.m. and ended by early afternoon. The curriculum focused on scripture, theology, church history, pastoral theology, ethics, and apologetics. Evensong was at 6:00 p.m., followed by dinner.

We took our meals in a magnificent dining hall called the refectory with high wooden beams and a grand marble fireplace with the words "Manners Maketh Man" inscribed on its mantel. It was an all-male school of about 200 students in those years.

The Episcopal Church is far more progressive than the Pentecostal tradition in which I was raised, and our theological training reflected the difference. We read the scriptures with open minds, aware that they were written by many different authors with little scientific knowledge but deep moral insight. Unlike Pentecostals, we didn't take the Bible literally. We approached biblical writings as symbol and metaphor. The words of scripture were seen as the beginning of wisdom and understanding, not their end.

New York in the 1960s was a fascinating time and place to be young. People were stacked in high-rise apartments like hotcakes, and we could hear their voices coming through the windows as we walked past. Sometimes we'd see fighting in the streets. Life below soaring skyscrapers—even in dicier neighborhoods like our own—was exhilarating for a young man who'd spent most of his life in a far less stimulating environment. My head was spinning as I reeled from one activity to another. My introduction to the cultural life of New York often came about through invitations from older gentlemen I met through the seminary or the parish church where I did my field work. Thanks to their generosity and tutelage, I soon discovered the glories of the city's theaters, musical concerts, art galleries and museums.

Little did I know I was developing a reputation as one skilled in the art of seduction. I was an insecure young man who wanted to be liked, so I used all the charm I could muster to make that happen. I didn't realize this sometimes evoked far stronger feelings than I'd intended. A number of my fellow seminarians had gone to Ivy League schools. They intimidated me with their sophistication.

Matters came to a head when one of the upperclassmen fell in love with me and broke off his engagement to his fiancée. I was not sexually attracted to him although I very much desired a close relationship to him, but was baffled by the intensity of his feelings.

Word of this incident got around, and several people accused me of deliberately trying to seduce the upperclassman. Their condemnation drove me into such a crisis of my own that I went to see the psychiatrist hired by the seminary to work with its students. I felt rejected and falsely maligned. I wrote a letter to my bishop and said I was going to leave seminary. I didn't yet understand that my efforts to charm could be unwittingly manipulative and lead to unwelcome consequences that were hurtful to me and to others. The psychiatrist helped me to become more conscious of what I was doing, which ended up serving me well in the years to come as a priest. Ultimately the upperclassman and I reconnected and became good friends.

There were other gay students at the seminary, and several of the tutors and faculty lecturers were homosexual. Our need to remain closeted to avoid expulsion or dismissal was psychologically unhealthy. Change was in the wind, however, and our lives gradually improved. The latter 1960s were a time of great social change, and the breezes of reform came to the General Seminary my second year with the arrival of the new dean, Samuel J. Wylie. Dean Wylie declared an "open policy" regarding sexual orientation at the seminary. I was a member of the student advisory committee appointed to draft the details of the new approach. We recommended that the policy include a "non-predatory" clause stipulating that ordained priests, "whether gay or straight," should not engage in predatory behavior with the laity. Our intention was to discontinue past practice in which only gay students and clergy were singled out for negative judgment and instead to apply positive behavioral norms to homosexual and heterosexual priests alike.

While the new policy created a less threatening atmosphere for gay people in the seminary, it had little effect on the church beyond its precincts. Few gay seminarians ever informed their bishops of the fact, and even fewer came out to their congregations. Such repression sometimes carried a tragic cost. I knew of at least three bishops whose sons committed suicide after struggling with their sexual orientations. One had recently been in seminary with me. He took a boat out into the Caribbean and shot himself.

Dealing with my sexual orientation wasn't the only challenge I faced. Divinity students were exempted from the draft and military service in Vietnam along with the mentally ill and "perverts." Although I was glad not to have to fight in a war I considered immoral, I felt guilty to be spared when others, less fortunate, were not. In the evenings after chapel, a group of us would watch the war news to see what was happening. The Vietnam coverage was increasingly critical and beginning to shock the country. The raw video footage affected me deeply. Steve Banger, a former college classmate who'd been in the Canterbury House dorm with me at Southern Illinois University, was killed in Vietnam that year. I felt helpless.

In my second year of seminary in 1967, I heard Martin Luther King, Jr. speak at Manhattan's Hunter College. There were only about a hundred of us in the audience, and I was quite taken with him. He came out strongly against the war because so many young black men without student deferments were being sent into harm's way—and for what? Federal Bureau of Investigation Director J. Edgar Hoover was furious with King, and many of us later believed King was assassinated because of his anti-war stance. Boxing champion Muhammad Ali expressed his opposition to the war eloquently: "No, I am not going ten thousand miles from home to help murder and burn another poor nation simply to continue the domination of white slave masters of the darker people the world over. This is the day when such evils must come to an end." He later added, "No Vietnamese ever called me nigger."

The contrast between the elegant, protected close of the seminary and the surrounding working-class neighborhood was stark and thought-provoking. The disparity stood out in bold relief when bishops and rectors of prominent Episcopal parishes across the country arrived for Board of Trustee meetings, and their chauffeured limousines lined up along 9th Avenue. I became increasingly aware of the rarified atmosphere I lived in and how cloistered we were from ordinary life. I'd made a long leap from the coal fields of Southern Illinois, and the transition was occasionally disorienting. I decided early on never to forget my humble beginnings, and I've stuck to that commitment. Returning to my roots continues to be a grounding experience, even as I remain glad for the choices I made to move beyond them.

CHAPTER EIGHT

CHICAGO

In the spring of my senior year at seminary, I interviewed for a staff position with Father Joe Howell, rector of St. Augustine's Episcopal Church in Wilmette, Illinois, an upper-middle class suburb on the north shore of Chicago. Joe invited me to dinner with members of the vestry so that we could get to know each other. At one point, they asked me if I had any questions for them. "Well," I replied, "I'm aware there's been no mention of civil rights or the Vietnam war." I was keen to know where they stood and whether we'd make a good match. My question opened up a lively and engaging discussion, and I was delighted to discover they were willing to openly debate these complex issues. When I learned Joe had marched with Martin Luther King, Jr. in Chicago the year before, I thought, "These are my kind of people." The feeling must have been mutual, because Joe offered me the job right out of seminary, and I accepted with delight.

I began my ministry at St. Augustine's as soon as I was ordained deacon in June of 1968. The new job paid $10,000 a year and included housing in a one-bedroom apartment. The parish also provided a car allowance that came in handy for gassing up the Volkswagen Beetle my parents had bought me as a seminary graduation gift. Yes, my wonderful parents gave me a brand-new car, even though I'd chosen to be ordained in a tradition many Pentecostals viewed unfavorably.

I drove that Beetle back and forth from Chicago to Herrin many times, and it was like driving a washing machine. I had to press the pedal to the floorboard to accelerate. I was always in a hurry. In wintertime, the wind would almost blow the car off the road. Passing a semi-trailer was taking my life in my hands because its suction threatened to pull a small car like mine under its wheels. The six-hour drive would become increasingly hazardous as my eyes grew sleepy and my arms grew tired from all the hard steering. When it rained, the wipers could barely keep up with clearing the windshield. How I survived those trips, I don't know. Still, that little Beetle was my first car ever, and I loved it.

After six months as a deacon, I was ordained to the priesthood shortly before Christmas by the Bishop of Chicago, James Montgomery. As a priest, I could now consecrate the bread and wine of the Holy Communion before giving them to parishioners at the altar rail. The first time I gave communion at St. Augustine's, I noticed that almost all the men had soft, pink hands. The exception was a mechanic with the calloused hands I recognized from my working-class childhood. The sight of those hands always reminded me of how far I had come.

I served on the staff of St. Augustine's for almost five years. It was a richly rewarding experience and honed my skills as a parish priest. After five years, however, I was ready to do something different. I entered a training program for hospital chaplains in Chicago and spent the next three and a half years earning thirteen quarters of Clinical Pastoral Education credits at Rush-Presbyterian-St. Luke's Medical Center. That level of clinical experience would prove to be invaluable training for the challenges that lay ahead. I just didn't know it yet.

I'd met my partner, Terry, in the summer of 1975. About the same time that my chaplaincy training program drew to a close in Chicago, Terry was offered a very good job with the government in Washington, D.C. The timing was right, so I took my chances and followed him to begin a new life in our nation's capital.

CHAPTER NINE

Washington D.C.

The airport serving Washington, D.C. is on the Virginia side of the Potomac, and the view crossing into the city is exceptionally beautiful. The river widens at that point, and the vista takes in the Capitol building, the Washington Monument, the Jefferson Memorial, and the Lincoln Memorial. To the northwest, the Washington National Cathedral dominates the skyline from the highest hill in the city. On a ridge along the Virginia side of the river, the Robert E. Lee Memorial mansion overlooks Arlington Cemetery and the eternal flame above the grave of former President John F. Kennedy. President Lyndon Johnson loved the view so much that he designated a park—named after himself, of course—from which to take advantage of this spectacular panorama.

Terry and I bought a house on E Street along the southeast edge of Capitol Hill in a not-so-great neighborhood with a lot of crime. That's probably why we got a good deal on it. Terry's parents lived in suburban Washington, and he'd spent part of his boyhood there. Terry was very much at home in our nation's capital. For me, it was all new and exciting. I loved the history and the political energy of the place. When I'd started college at Southern Illinois University in 1960, my goal had been to become a lawyer and then a congressman, with the hope of making positive changes in the world. Now, although I was a priest and not a politician, Washington seemed just the place to be. Unlike Terry, I didn't have a job lined up when we moved, but I'd had extensive training in hospital chaplaincy and years of experience as a parish priest.

Even so, I sometimes worried that I wouldn't find work in

my chosen profession. I'd been a priest for eight years, and by that time I'd decided I would not live a lie. I was gay, and I was no longer willing to hide it, even though living in the closet had been the only way for homosexual clergy to survive for centuries. Coming out of the closet was a gamble. Being an openly gay priest meant there would be challenges ahead for me that others would not have to face.

Once we got settled on Capitol Hill, Terry's career took off. He spent his days designing and redesigning government offices. Sometimes that meant traveling all over the world. As busy as he was, his talent spilled over into our modest townhouse. Terry's taste ran to making things lush, plush, and elaborate. His ideal in interior design was Versailles—gilt and rococo, little pillows with fluffy trim. He marbleized the floors and painted murals on the walls. Our "mini-Versailles" townhouse became a point of considerable good-natured humor among our friends. When we actually did visit Versailles several years later, Terry called out, "I'm home!"

As for me, I'd always had a green thumb. As a child, I spent many happy hours planting flowers in our large backyard garden alongside my father, who put in nothing but vegetables. In Washington there was only a small plot of land in front of our townhouse to serve as a garden, but the flowers and I made the most of it.

Terry's parents and his gay brother and his partner lived nearby, so we celebrated all of the holidays and traditional occasions together as a family. We developed a wide circle of friends and soon became part of the gay social set, most of whom were in the closet. We hosted a black-tie dinner party every New Year's Eve and three or four Halloween costume parties renowned for their inventiveness. At my 40th birthday party in 1982, we jammed 80 people into our house and garden.

Whenever we partied, Terry and I would drink, and I would drink more. I soon realized that we'd developed a pattern: We'd go partying, I'd get drunk, and then we'd get into a fight on the way home. The next day, I'd never remember the substance of our arguments, but they could become quite animated. It took me a while to realize the part my drinking was playing in our interactions. It wasn't as if I'd down a 40-ounce bottle of vodka at one sitting, but it wasn't uncommon for me to get drunk frequently. Once I started, I always drank to get drunk. I liked the feeling of relinquishing responsibility.

My Pentecostal family were teetotalers, so I'd never been around alcohol until I got to college. That's where I began my long-term relationship with booze. I got drunk on beer for the first time at the age of 18, and I loved it. I remember lying on the bed with my head swimming and giggling with delight. I loved the feeling of being out of control but tried not to let it influence my professional life. I maintained my respect for the sanctity of the pulpit.

Terry and I would always party on Friday nights and sometimes on Saturday. I never drank on a Saturday night if I was scheduled to preach the next morning. Preaching or not, however, we usually started drinking at brunch after church on Sunday and continued through the rest of the day. Then on Monday, Tuesday, and Wednesday, I'd sober up. If we were on vacation, we partied every day. I did a lot of swimming to burn off the alcohol, but drinking was taking its toll. I was in denial.

It took me a couple of years to find a position in the Episcopal Church after our move to Washington, but I soon found secular work in the press office of Illinois Senator Adlai E. Stevenson, III and later as a campaign worker for a political candidate back in Illinois. I remain grateful for the opportunity these experiences gave me to realize a small portion of my earlier dream of getting involved in political life, but they reassured me that I really belonged in priestly work.

In the fall of 1979, I had lunch with an old friend, Jim Steen, the new rector of St. Patrick's Church in Northwest Washington, D.C. Jim and I had been friends in seminary, but I hadn't seen him for many years. Over lunch, he told me he needed help and invited me to come to work for him. I began to cry. At last, I was being offered an opportunity to return to active ministry.

Compared to surrounding parishes, St. Patrick's was relatively progressive. Jim hired another priest, Steve Davenport, at the same time, and we became a dynamic team, ultimately growing the congregation and raising funds for a much-needed larger church, which we then built. It was and is a beautiful structure.

Jim funded my part-time position, which paid the princely

sum of $6,000 per year, by renting out Sunday School rooms during the week to the newly established Selma Levine School of Music. Membership and tithes had declined during the tenure of St. Patrick's previous rector, and Jim had been brought in to revive the upper-middle class congregation. Jim was certainly up to the task, and, if I do say so myself, he chose wisely in hiring Steve and me.

By January of 1981, things were going so well that the parish decided they needed a full-time assistant rector. Although Jim had been able to hire me part-time on his own authority, the vestry—lay leaders elected to help conduct parish business—had to approve funding for the new full-time position. Naturally, I thought I was made for the job, and I wanted it badly. At the same time, I was no longer willing to present myself as anything other than I was, a well-trained, experienced Episcopal priest who happened to be gay. I would not hide the fact that I lived with my partner and lover, Terry. I would not live a lie any longer.

CHAPTER TEN

COMING OUT

Coming out of the closet can take a lifetime for many gay men, even when they realize that they're gay at an early age, and even when they're courageous enough to reveal their sexual identity to the people they love. But it's not only to loved ones that we come out; we sometimes have to come out to relative strangers, especially in work situations. Sometimes it seems we're never allowed to stop coming out. Occasionally, it's not a problem, but more often it's a matter of waiting in isolation and silence for the other shoe to drop.

Of course, it's more than a shoe we're waiting for. We're waiting to see whether it's tied to bigotry and discrimination and will kick us hard where it hurts. My decision to live openly as a gay man was a gradual process. The prospect of revealing my homosexuality to family, friends, and colleagues was daunting for many years.

During the early years of my parish ministry in Wilmette, I'd pretended to be straight. Such duplicity took an inordinate amount of energy, especially when coupled with the fear that the truth would be discovered and my life ruined. There were parishioners who advised me that I needed to get married to advance my career in the Church.

After five years in parish ministry, I'd entered a training program for hospital chaplains in Chicago. A wise mentor there saved my life and my ministry by gently pointing out how much anger I was carrying and suggested I see a psychotherapist for counseling. My three subsequent years of therapy were instrumental in making it possible for me to accept myself and live openly as a gay man.

The first issue we addressed was how angry I was with my father for "making" me gay. My father was a faithful, steady provider for my family and was deeply in love with our mother. Sadly, he was emotionally reserved with his children, especially me. He was not physically affectionate, and I desperately wanted that. It was easy for me to buy into the popular myth floating around that overly protective mothers and emotionally distant fathers were the leading causes of homosexuality in boys. Once I stopped blaming my dad for making me gay, I came to the realization that in fact it was God that had made me that way. This was a relief for me, and it gave me a tremendous sense of freedom.

The other major issue that got resolved in my psychotherapy was letting go of the drive to get married and raise a family. I had grown up in a family where my parents loved each other very much and excelled at married life. When parents are very accomplished in a particular area, sometimes that lays a heavy burden on the children. This was true of me with my drive to get married and father seven children. I had declared that's how many children I wanted. Of course, there were no gay marriages back then to offer an alternative option. Because I was able to reconcile these issues with my sexual identity within my own soul, I was able then to fall in love with Terry Parsons and settle down in a committed relationship for thirteen years.

I came out to my family in 1974 at the age of 32. Specifically, I came out to my younger sister, Norma Jean, at three o'clock in the morning after fortifying myself with hefty doses of bourbon. Her gentle reply was anticlimactic. "Well," she said, "you haven't told me anything we don't already know." I was shocked. I thought I'd been protecting them from my dreadful secret all my life. I've observed a well-established phenomenon over the intervening years: Mothers always seem to know. Even so, none of us had ever discussed it openly.

I asked Norma to take the information back to our family in Herrin. I'd never felt judged by my family, and that didn't change after I brought the truth out into the open. Soon after my coming-out conversation with Norma Jean, I heard from my older sister, Thelma Imogene, and her husband, Bob. They wrote me the most beautiful, accepting and affirming letter. It made a huge difference in my ability to accept myself.

I've treasured that letter for years. Thelma was like a second mother to me and Norma Jean. When I left the Pentecostal tradition for the Episcopal Church and came under fire from my boyhood church for leaving the "true faith," Thelma was there to defend me. Unlike too many other families I encountered during my later AIDS ministry, my family understood what it meant to love. It's not that we all got together for a Kumbaya moment. In fact, we never went in for that sort of display, and we didn't talk much about the details of my sexual orientation. But with Thelma's letter, it was clear that my family loved me just as I was and not as I'd imagined they always wanted me to be.

Coming out to my family was exhilarating. I felt the lifting of a great burden; I'd "laid it down," as scripture says. It was tremendously liberating to be myself. I'd thrown off the heavy cloak of denial I'd been dragging around all my life. When the time came for the vestry at St. Patrick's to make its decision about a full-time assistant rector, I wasn't about to get that cloak out of the closet again—not even to secure a job I wanted with all my heart. When I'd first attended an Episcopal service with its hallowed traditions and beautiful liturgy back in college, I knew I'd found my spiritual home. I knew now that the only way I could serve the church with authenticity and integrity as a priest was to disclose my homosexuality to the vestry, to the congregation, and to the bishop.

This was a risky step. The screening process had kept some of my contemporaries from ever going to seminary in the first place because of their homosexuality. Other gay men who were ordained later left the church in frustration at having to live a lie. Some were fired by their parishes for trying to lead authentic lives. If they were lucky, they found a decent line of work in the secular world, perhaps in teaching, counseling, or administration. Since that wasn't their original intention, many of these men became bitter and left the church completely.

Before applying for the full-time position at St. Patrick's, I made it clear to the rector that I wanted the vestry to make its decision knowing that I was gay and that I was living in a committed relationship with another man. Jim and I agreed that Bishop Walker should also have all of the facts before making me canonically resident in the Diocese of Washington and fully subject to his jurisdiction.

After our conversation, Jim talked with the vestry and informed Bishop Walker of my status. To my lasting good fortune, both the vestry and the bishop quietly welcomed me into the diocese as an openly gay man. Although low-key, this was a historic moment. Back in the Diocese of Springfield, Illinois, where I'd been baptized and confirmed, there were no openly gay priests. If I'd come out there, I'd never have been given work. I was the first Episcopal priest to come out as openly gay in the Washington D.C. Diocese and was fortunate to be accepted and allowed to exercise my priesthood.

Complicating the selection process for the full-time job at St. Patrick's, the Episcopal Church had authorized the ordination of women priests in 1976. I was a feminist and strongly supported the ordination of women, but it had never occurred to me that I might one day be competing with them for a job. Before Jim was hired by the vestry as rector, some members of the congregation had wanted a woman to lead the parish. I was chagrined to find myself selfishly worried that the vestry might overlook the success I'd had with the parish to date and choose a woman instead.

Bishop Gene Robinson, the first openly gay bishop consecrated in the Episcopal Church, has often remarked that in the large house of misogyny, there's a small room of homophobia. Homophobia is often characterized by fear of the anima, the feminine aspect of the psyche that resides in all persons. Many homophobes hate the feminine in gay men because they feel it perverts their notions of a pure masculine ideal. They are often invested in the traditional anthropomorphic portrayal of God as male and oppose the ordination of women to the priesthood.

My support for the feminist cause was also strategic. There's strength in numbers, and by supporting women in their struggle, gay men could hope to attract potential allies for the gay cause. When women found acceptance in the priesthood before homosexuals, however, I couldn't escape the irony: Women had successfully challenged the traditional patriarchy, and I was part and parcel of that system even though it personally condemned me as a gay man.

The vestry's meeting to choose St. Patrick's new assistant rapidly turned into a knock-down, drag-out argument that lasted far into the night. I sat by the phone at home and waited to learn their decision. Tired of holding his breath, Terry had gone to bed, so Dorothy and I kept each other company as I waited anxiously for Jim to call me with the news. Dorothy, our tabby cat, was so homely she was cute. We had rescued her from the alley behind our townhouse where there were too many cats, dogs, and rats.

Finally, shortly after midnight, the telephone rang. Jim relayed the events of the meeting over the phone. It had been stormy and inconclusive. Some of the parishioners wanted a woman priest. Others were worried about the optics of hiring a gay priest to run the youth group, a key responsibility of the incoming assistant rector. I'd had a great deal of experience running a youth ministry back in Chicago, so my ability to do so responsibly and ethically weren't seriously in doubt. Still, they hadn't been able to resolve their concerns, so the meeting came to a temporary halt. The vestry decided that they would spend two weeks discussing the new position with their fellow parishioners. Following this informal poll, they would reconvene and make their decision.

Those next two weeks were challenging and instructive. Although anxious about the final outcome, I was fascinated to watch the parish struggle with this issue. I sensed that the older folks and the youngsters were my strongest supporters while the middle-aged crowd had more reservations and leaned against my appointment. I wasn't sure, though.

To my great relief, Jim called at the end of the vestry's final vote to tell me that I'd been chosen as St. Patrick' new full-time assistant rector. That evening, the staff with whom I'd been working for the past few years threw a party for me at Jim's house, and we celebrated my hiring in high spirits.

Given the controversy over my hiring, I did feel insecure in taking on my new role at the very beginning. It was my turn to preach the Sunday after the vestry's decision. When I ascended the pulpit, I felt unexpectedly vulnerable and exposed as I stood before the congregation. Just as feelings of anxiety threatened to overwhelm me, a small voice whispered within, "They're not running away. Relax." I'd been fantasizing about this moment for years, and now it had become reality. I'd finally been chosen for their team.

The youth ministry at St. Patrick's wasn't as large as the one I'd built in Chicago, where I'd been able to engage young people in a variety of activities. The kids at St. Patrick's came from different schools around the Washington area, so we were mostly limited to Sunday morning gatherings. We did take occasional ski trips and a couple of weekend trips to New York City, accompanied by a handful of adult chaperones. One time, we stayed in the Cathedral of St. John the Divine, bunking in the undercroft in sleeping bags with a couple hundred other teenagers. On another visit, we went to see a Broadway play, Mass Appeal, which dealt with the relationship between a young liberal Catholic priest and an older, more conservative priest. I wasn't sure what the play was about, but, fortunately, the group had chosen it without my input. It turned out that one of the themes was homosexuality. It was fascinating to watch this play about accepting gay priests with my parishioners, knowing it would make them think. One of the chaperones had considered hiring me a risk because he had three sons in the youth group. I like to think the play opened his mind and heart at least a little.

Despite its progressive leanings, St. Patrick's needed time to get used to having an openly gay priest on its staff.

Parishioners sometimes found it awkward to deal with the issue directly. Soon after I was hired, the vestry's secretary called to ask if I'd be offended if he used the word "homosexual" when writing up the minutes of the meeting that had decided my fate. "Well, that's what we're talking about, isn't it?" I replied with a smile.

I had to laugh. After all, I was a homosexual priest, so if they had to record what their debate had been about, then that's what they should say. In his inexperience and discomfort with the topic, the secretary was feeling understandably uncomfortable.

Early on, I'd been told that I was most definitely not to talk about homosexuality from the pulpit. The rector told me that directly, but I suspect it originated with the vestry's Senior Warden. Even though they'd voted me in, they were cautious about making any "great leaps forward."

One of the great things about coming out at St. Patrick's was that Terry was fully recognized as my partner, and he became an active member of the parish. He sang in the choir and served on the interior design committee for the new church building. We socialized with many of the parishioners, and it meant a lot to us to be accepted as a couple. Terry was happy with the church, with our circle of friends, and in his work for the government. Terry's father was a diplomat, so Terry had grown up in various locations around the globe. He loved to travel. He worked on remodeling the Talleyrand Mansion which housed the government offices in Paris and on other prestigious buildings. During the first year of Ronald Reagan's presidency, Terry was assigned to assist the designer at the White House for the better part of a year, and I got a quick private tour of the place, including the Oval Office. Terry was in hog heaven, as we say back in Herrin.

My relationship with Terry was a comfort and an inspiration in those years. Our commitment ran deep, as was common among the gay couples we knew. Without the blessing of the church or the support of the state, we had only ourselves to guard the sanctity and integrity of our relationships. Without the value I placed on my relationship with Terry, I doubt I would have been prepared to risk falling on my sword professionally, as I did in coming out to the congregation at St. Patrick's. I didn't want to disrespect the love we shared by failing to acknowledge it or lying about it. I wanted us to have the same respect accorded to my parents' marriage and the freedom to be open about it.

Although I'd been accepted as a gay priest by the people at St. Patrick's and the Bishop of Washington, the Episcopal Church's Virginia Theological Seminary, just across the Potomac River in Alexandria, Virginia banned me from supervising its students during their field education in the parish. This meant that the other priests at St. Patrick's could supervise a student's field training, but I alone could not because I was gay.

John Walker, Bishop of the Diocese of Washington, could have been more aggressive in supporting me against the seminary, but he was walking a political tightrope of his own. He was African American and had been the first black student to graduate from the Virginia Seminary in the 1950s. Later, he was the first black canon at the Washington National Cathedral. There's no doubt he understood prejudice. He was himself a pioneer.

The year 1981 wasn't an easy time for Bishop Walker to tackle any issues associated with homosexuality within the church. The same month the seminary banned me from supervising its seminarians, there was a meeting of the Anglican primates at his cathedral. These senior bishops from provinces around the world appeared to have an unspoken agreement to avoid any open discussion of homosexuality in the high counsels of Anglicanism. Anyone who tried to raise the topic publicly would meet considerable resistance marked by stony silence.

I was informed by one of the bishop's staff that he did not want to have to deal with a *Washington Post* story about homosexuality while the primates were in town. If my conflict with Virginia Seminary had gotten into the press, all Hell would have broken loose. That had to wait for better days.

It wasn't until years later, at the Lambeth Conference in London in 1988, that the primates would discuss the subject of homosexuality openly. When homosexual issues were finally placed on the table, they triggered a bitter, bloody battle resulting in the passage of repressive, anti-gay resolutions. At the same time, the Episcopal Church in the United States was moving toward greater inclusion of gay and lesbian people

Bishop Walker was also worried that if I fought the Seminary's ban, homophobes within the church might file morals charges against me. As far as they were concerned, my partner and I were living in sin. In my naiveté, the thought of an ecclesiastical trial hadn't occurred to me. I was much more vulnerable than I'd imagined. I thought I'd found a safe home when hired by St. Patrick's. I'd assumed that acceptance by my parish and diocesan bishop translated into acceptance by the national Episcopal Church. I was mistaken.

The mere hint of a morals charge brought home the realization that the yoke of prejudice still lay firmly across my back. The ordeal of an ecclesiastical trial was a frightening prospect. Bishop Walker probably had my best interests at heart, but I'm not sure he fully got the importance of gay people living openly with self-acceptance. Still, he'd said yes to my coming out to St. Patrick's parish, and the parish gave me a great gift by inviting and accepting my ministry as a gay priest. After all the years of closeted self-loathing, I could now live with integrity and pride.

At times of stress when feeling discouraged, I did find support and reassurance from other quarters. After the Virginia Seminary banned me from supervising its seminarians, I was invited to tea by Verna Dozier, a deeply spiritual, older African American woman who was a lay preacher and teacher in the Episcopal Church. She wrote books and led retreats, and she was greatly admired.

Verna put my situation in perspective. Over tea, she told me about her own experiences with discrimination:

"Jerry," she said "when my friends and I were growing up,

we were told that if we scrubbed ourselves real clean, and if we got a good education and spoke English just like the Queen of England, white people would like us. I believed that for a while. But when we did grow up, even following that advice, we found that some white people weren't going to like us regardless of what we did. They found it quite easy, in fact, to hate us."

She spoke as one who had undergone great trials and triumphed gloriously.

CHAPTER ELEVEN

1984 and the Epidemic Continues

Bill, our first close friend in Washington, D.C. to succumb to AIDS, died in the summer of 1983 soon after my visit with Jack Harris in San Francisco when I'd heard about the sudden deaths of his parishioners and friends. Bill didn't have an easy death, and watching him die was dreadful. His mother and sister were there when I visited him in the hospital, and they were distraught by his condition. Bill was flailing against his restraints and groaning loudly as he twisted and turned on his bed.

I'd been a priest for fifteen years by then, had completed three and a half years of clinical training as a hospital chaplain, and had been present with many people as they faced death. None of that prepared me for what I was seeing now. I was overwhelmed by despair as I witnessed Bill's suffering, and words failed as I tried to comfort his family. I was deeply humbled by this experience and even now find it difficult to write about how paralyzed and impotent I felt. Bill died that same week without ever recovering his sanity.

Bill's death was soon followed by that of a priest friend, Mills, and of another close friend, Larry, not long after that.

Others faced similar losses all around me. One afternoon, three young men and a woman approached me about their friend, Darryl, a 28-year-old man dying in a hospice just across the river in Northern Virginia. They wanted to plan a memorial service and asked if I'd help them. It soon became apparent that we were navigating troubled waters. They felt tension with Darryl's parents and did not know how to proceed. I offered to visit Darryl in the hospice and to meet his mom and dad.

I was shocked by Darryl's condition. He'd wasted away to skin and bones. His skin was blackened with cancerous lesions, and he was unable to communicate. Never before had I seen a body so deteriorated yet still alive. Darryl's parents were beside themselves. His mother, a nurse, was practically hysterical. She recounted how, a few days earlier, she'd been in an emergency room and gotten blood on her hands from a male patient. On seeing this, another nurse had run over and urged her to scrub her hands, exclaiming, "Oh my God, he may have AIDS! He may have AIDS!" Darryl's mother, knowing she was about to visit her own son who was dying of AIDS, was speechless.

Darryl's parents were open to discussing their son's memorial service, but it was tough going all the way. Burdened by her sorrow, Darryl's mother resisted most of my suggestions. She declared that if we sang a particular hymn—any hymn—under those circumstances, she'd never be able to sing it again. The same went for any passage of scripture I recommended.

I suggested that the structure of the service be informal and allow an opportunity for Darryl's friends to stand up and talk about what his life had meant to them. At that point, his mother threw me a troubled look and asked, "Will anybody say he was gay? His brother will be there and he's only 17. I don't want him to know he's gay."

"Well, I can't tell you what people are going to say," I replied, "but I guarantee you they'll be respectful." She got up in tears and ran out of the room, leaving me and her husband to take care of the details.

Afterwards, I got in my car and drove back into Washington where I was supposed to lead an evening study group at the church. I cried all the way to the meeting and, once I got there, it was all I could do not to continue weeping in frustration and sorrow. They tried to put me back together.

Darryl's memorial service proved to be a healing means of grace. Twenty-seven people attended. We sat together in a circle with Darryl's ashes in an urn at the center. We sang hymns and read passages of scripture, and people talked about what Darryl had meant to them. The mother and father were there with the 17-year-old brother, and nobody said the word "gay." Midway through the service, everybody relaxed, and the mourners experienced an emotional and spiritual shift. Darryl's memorial gathering became a love-fest. People spoke of Darryl with warmth and affection, and we had a lovely reception afterwards.

This was new territory. I'd been flying by the seat of my pants in putting the service together and couldn't be certain how it would all come together. In the end it was a great success and a blessing to all who attended. We'd done our best to help that family and each other come to terms with our grief at losing Darryl, and our best turned out to be very good indeed.

Bringing together Darryl's family and friends made me think of a long-ago science fiction film in which spaceships from rival worlds had to dock at the same port for an intergalactic peace conference. The disparate groups didn't know or trust each other at the beginning, but they had a common cause. In "docking" for Darryl's memorial service, emissaries from both his worlds united to celebrate the life of their son, their brother, and their friend. I didn't realize it until later, but this was to become a pattern, a template for many other memorial services yet to come.

CHAPTER TWELVE

Leaving St. Patrick's

My years at St. Patrick's passed swiftly. I'd done good work providing pastoral care for the elderly, making hospital visits, and officiating at funerals and weddings. We'd worked hard to strengthen the congregation and build the new church, just two blocks from the old one.

By the summer of 1985, I was riding the crest of a wave, both personally and professionally. Terry and I had sold our townhouse on Capitol Hill and bought a house in Alexandra, Virginia, just across the Potomac. Our new residence was a freestanding, colonial brick house with dormer windows and a spacious garden. The garden held eight flower beds that had gone to seed, and I was to have the time of my life reviving them.

The house was located in a gracious old neighborhood on a quiet street with friendly neighbors, mostly retirees and young families with children. It was also in the most liberal voting district in the region.

Our new neighbors threw a welcoming party for us when we moved in. I could hardly believe our good fortune. This was a far cry from the crime-ridden street in D.C. where our house had been burglarized twice, and Terry had been mugged at knifepoint at the front door. From my small office on the second floor of our new home, I could see across the river to the dome of the Capitol building. I could have lived there forever and thought that I would. It seemed our dreams were coming true.

On June 1, 1985, we dedicated St. Patrick's new church building. Helping to build that church was one of the great joys of my life. A thousand people attended the service, and we processed en masse up the two blocks from our old building to the spectacular new structure, which featured an elegant post-modern design. Bishop Walker, who'd approved my serving as an openly gay priest just four years before, officiated at the ceremony.

The following week, riding high on the success of our move to the new building, I took twenty parishioners on a pilgrimage to Israel. Our rector, Jim Steen, accompanied us, as did Susan Gressinger, who was ordained to the priesthood in the National Cathedral on the morning of our departure. Susan's ordination had some dramatic moments when protesters disrupted the service. Her husband was a medical doctor who had worked for Family Planning, so the protesters were there to smear her as pro-abortion. Standing together at the airport, Susan and I watched the protests on the news as we awaited our departure for Israel. Shortly afterwards we boarded our flight, and within hours we were in Jerusalem.

Jerusalem is a fascinating place with narrow, winding streets hallowed by history and legend. There was something new and exciting to see around every corner. Near the end of our trip, Jim Steen and I wandered through the old city together, just the two of us. Jim seemed uncharacteristically subdued. When we stopped for dinner, it was clear he needed to talk, and it had something to do with St. Patrick's recently elected vestry. At regular intervals, the parish elected new lay leaders to serve on the vestry, and earlier that spring the old vestry that had guided us so well for nearly six years had been replaced with new members.

Over dinner and without preamble, Jim announced, "The new leadership is worried about money and the expense of the new church." This was news to me. "Now that we've built the new church," he continued, "we've got this big mortgage, and they want to cut back on the budget. One of the easiest places to cut is your salary." This came totally out of the blue. He'd blindsided me far away from home, and I felt the earth shift. I was in shock and at a complete loss for words.

As we flew back to Washington, this pilgrim was far less exuberant than when he'd departed. How could this be happening after all the great work we'd done? I held my breath for several days, hoping that Jim would express disagreement with the officers' decision, or that they'd change their minds. Instead, within two weeks, the new Senior Warden, Joan Kingdom, invited me to dinner at her house where the other officers of the vestry had gathered. They were all people I'd gotten to know very well, and with whom I'd socialized regularly, but I was apprehensive. Over dinner—I could barely get anything down—Joan carefully explained why they were letting me go. It was all about saving money and paying the mortgage. No matter how she phrased it, I was out. I went into the bathroom and threw up. Then I left.

Word spread through the congregation, and many people were furious at the vestry's decision. Some wanted me to fight to stay, and a few actually left the parish in protest. I'd seen other churches become divided over staffing decisions, and it can be awful. I didn't want that for St. Patrick's. It would have been a mess if I'd fought to stay on, and I doubt I'd have won. I'd been around long enough to know that if you're an assistant priest and the rector doesn't fight to keep you, it's time to go.

I was confident I'd made a positive contribution to the life of St. Patrick's. The congregation had grown significantly during the six years I was there. In the summer of 1979, I'd celebrated a Sunday mass there as a fill-in priest. Fewer than ten people attended the early mass, and around 40 attended the later service. By contrast, in 1985 by the time I was fired, a typical mass would have 200 people in attendance. Our growth was a major success story.

My sexual orientation undoubtedly played a part in the vestry's decision to fire me. The first woman we baptized in the new church was a lesbian, and by the time I left St. Patrick's, 31 gay men and lesbians had become members of the parish. They felt they'd found a safe space to share their faith in a parish willing to hire an openly gay priest. I suspect this was unsettling to any number of the straight members of the parish. One gay man or lesbian in the congregation was a novelty, but several constituted a threat. They didn't want St. Patrick's to become a "gay" church.

Perhaps having so many gay members sparked fears of contagion once the AIDS epidemic hit its stride. In those early years, nobody was sure exactly how the disease was transmitted or how much risk it posed to the general population. Ignorance and paranoia abounded on all sides.

Strange as it may seem, Terry's and my relationship was the most stable of the relationships of the priests on staff at St. Patrick's. The other clergy had divorced their wives, so I had to question the value judgments underlying the vestry's decision. In any event, the only reason I was given for my dismissal was that it was an economic move to save money.

Leaving St. Patrick's left me worried and depressed. I don't think Jim and the vestry realized in firing me just how difficult it would be for me to find other work now that I was known as an openly gay priest. Neither, I sensed, did they fully appreciate the historic significance of having hired me in the first place.

We'd just bought our new house, and I had no idea if or when I'd be able to find another job in Washington. If I looked elsewhere, such as New York or San Francisco, what would Terry do? He was professionally moored in D.C., so we couldn't think of uprooting and moving someplace else. Fortunately, the vestry had given me a six-month salary package as a severance payment. This was a godsend, a generous and welcome gift. It gave me some breathing room.

By mid-January of 1986, I was finished at St. Patrick's. I'd come to the end of six of the most creative and exciting years of my life, and I faced an uncertain future.

CHAPTER THIRTEEN

IN THE WILDERNESS

I had a small reserve of cash but no job prospects and spent my days wondering what to do with myself. I felt I'd been cast into the wilderness, a sacrificial lamb. Despite my sense of betrayal, I tried not to despair. I'd lived long enough by age 44 to believe that if this had happened, something more promising must be on the way. I had to hope circumstances would lead me beyond my fear. My Pentecostal upbringing had taught me that when we seek God in the wilderness, God will find us. I fell back on this belief whenever I found myself despairing. I'd been lost, and I'd been found before. It would happen again. This conviction gave me courage and hope as events unfolded over the next year or so.

Following my dismissal from St. Patrick's, four laymen from the congregation volunteered to help me find a job. They wrote a letter to the Bishop of Virginia, Peter Lee, to introduce me and to outline my qualifications. They asked if he would meet with me to discuss possible job opportunities in the Virginia Diocese. I was grateful for their efforts on my behalf, but I didn't think much would come of it. Bishop Lee had been on the Board of Trustees of the Virginia Theological Seminary when it banned me from supervising their students.

Nevertheless, I made an appointment with the bishop and drove two hours to meet with him in Richmond. I was ushered into his antique-laden, historically appointed office where he wasted little time in preliminaries. "Jerry," he told me, "there isn't a single parish in the diocese that wouldn't discover what's going on in your personal life during the hiring process, and the one parish that might consider hiring you doesn't have a vacancy." He was most gracious and kind, but the result was the same; he confirmed what I already knew. I thanked him for his time and headed back home.

It was a gray, rainy day, and I tried not to despair as I made the return trip to Alexandria. Yet again, my inner resolve came to the rescue as I found myself singing a variation of the words from a favorite hymn, "'Tis grace has brought you safe thus far, and grace will lead you home." It was all the reassurance I needed. With wry amusement, I noted I was passing the exit for the Civil War battlefield where Confederate General Stonewall Jackson had died as a result of friendly fire from his own soldiers.

Help was on the way. Don Burnes and Alice Baum were an energetic couple who directed Samaritan Ministries, a religious organization that reached out to serve the needs of impoverished, often black, communities. I'd done some fundraising for them before, and that next summer of 1986 they offered me a job as a part-time Chaplain, giving me a renewed sense of energy and purpose.

In the meantime, I wasn't about to rest on my laurels. I needed full-time work and was enthused to learn that St. Margaret's Episcopal Church was looking for a new rector. The church was located in what was becoming the premier gay neighborhood around DuPont Circle in Washington, D.C. The area wasn't only gay, it was close to black and Latino communities, embassy residences, and historical homes. Former President and Mrs. Obama now own a house two blocks from the church. The rector who'd retired had been there for many years. To replace him, they'd hired one of the dullest priests on the face of the earth. After three years, they'd had enough and asked him to leave. I suppose if there's anything worse than being fired because you're gay, it's being fired because you're so boring no one can stand you. When I heard all this, some friends and I decided I'd be the perfect person to become the new rector, so we started a campaign.

It wasn't long before one of Bishop Walker's staffers, whom I knew, told me, "The bishop is not ready to have an openly gay priest and his lover living in one of his rectories." Not trusting the source, I initially dismissed this and mounted a full-on campaign. I soon received a polite letter from the bishop, however, in which he confirmed his staff's communication. The bishop made it clear that because of my public statement about my sexuality, my candidacy was unlikely to go anywhere. Soon after that, I heard through the grapevine that the lack of support wasn't originating so much from St. Margaret's search committee as it was from the bishop himself.

I doubt that Bishop Walker fully comprehended what the gay rights movement was about and how important it was that gay and lesbian individuals be able to live openly and with integrity. For him and for Bishop Lee, just over the Potomac in Virginia, negotiating their own political minefields was understandably their priority. But their priority wasn't my priority. I didn't give up my campaign to become the rector of St. Margaret's, and the lobbying on my behalf continued.

CHAPTER FOURTEEN

AIDS – The Deep End

August 26, 1986 was Terry's 40th birthday. He'd thrown a big 40th birthday party for me four years earlier, so I was planning a surprise birthday dinner for him at a fine French restaurant in downtown D.C. It was on a Tuesday night, and I'd invited 57 people, including my older sister, Thelma Imogene, and her husband, Bob, who were in town for a visit. I was excited about the celebration and had put in a lot of work to make sure everything went smoothly. Then, the morning of the party, I got a phone call telling me that Logan Sallada, a beloved friend, was in the intensive care unit at the George Washington Hospital. He was dying of AIDS.

Logan and I had been close friends since 1977 when he moved into the house next door to ours on Capitol Hill shortly after we arrived. He'd soon become the brother I'd lost when Ralph Waldo died fifteen months before I was born.

I grew up longing for an older brother to help fight my battles. My brother James was nearly 20 years older so wasn't around during my growing-up years. I didn't like to fight and wasn't any good in sports, but in our working-class neighborhood, I had to fight whether I wanted to or not. I had to step up to the plate. Although I'd never met Ralph Waldo, I used to think, "If only Ralph were here." When Logan moved in next door all those many years later, I found the brother I'd always wanted. And now he was dying.

Logan was a gay Republican, which meant, of course, that he was firmly in the closet. Although we argued endlessly about politics, we had a lot in common. We'd both been interested in government and public policy in college, but when I entered seminary in New York City, he entered the Peace Corps. I had seriously considered joining the Peace Corps myself. When Logan came out of the Peace Corps, he helped the ultraconservative political figure Pat Buchanan run the Youth for Nixon program during the 1968 presidential campaign. Buchanan was vehemently anti-gay and leaned far to the right on both religious and political issues—all good reasons for Logan to want to stay in the closet.

Logan had been briefly married before moving to Washington and was out to only a few gay friends. Following his divorce, he cut off straight friends from his past; he'd been appointed to a good job through Republican contacts and was afraid he might be publicly outed. His path into marriage may have been mine had I not gotten psychotherapeutic help.

Logan admired and envied Terry and me because we had a solid, committed relationship. He so wanted to settle down in a committed relationship but never seemed to be able to make it work. When Ronald Reagan was elected president, Logan's paranoia kicked into high gear. He heard a rumor that Reagan was going to close all the gay bars in D.C. I did my best to reassure him. "Logan," I said, "that's the craziest thing I've ever heard. Reagan's got gay friends in Hollywood. He's not going to worry about a few gay bars!"

In 1984, Logan was assigned to help with preparations for an international conference on the environment that was to be held in Versailles, so he moved to Paris for 18 months. I visited him there twice. At the end of 1985, he returned to Washington and moved in with a mutual friend. He frequented gay bars and clubs, but he wasn't out to his family or colleagues at work.

About a week before Logan was hospitalized, we'd gone out to dinner together. By that time, I was concerned about his health. His energy seemed to diminish. Most of my friends in the gay community were still in denial about AIDS. Perhaps the reality was just too hard to handle. It was difficult for me to bring up my concerns during our dinner conversation, but I did, and Logan became defensive. "No, no," he exclaimed. "I've talked to my doctor, and I don't have that." He swept the whole thing under the carpet.

Then came the morning of Terry's birthday party and the call that Logan had AIDS and was dying. I felt like lightening had struck at the heels of my boots. I raced down to the hospital, getting a traffic ticket on the way. I hurried into the intensive care unit and found Logan on oxygen. I was devastated. Although we'd never been lovers, I truly loved Logan and shared a deep bond with him. We were brothers.

As Logan struggled to breathe through his oxygen mask, he told me two things. He'd bought a gold Cartier watch at the U.S. Embassy gift shop in Paris, and it was a treasured possession. "I want you to have it," he said, "to remember all our good times in France." Then he said, "I want to live long enough to see you become the rector of St. Margaret's." He'd been one of the most vocal cheerleaders in my bid for that job.

To say I was upset when I left the hospital is an understatement. I needed to talk to someone, anyone, but when I stopped at a pay phone, I called a friend and began to sob. Things became a bit of a blur after that. Terry's birthday party was still on, but I was struggling over whether I should tell our friends what was happening with Logan. When I got home, I sent Thelma and Bob on ahead to the restaurant while Terry and I sat in the living room and cried as we toasted Logan and Terry's 40th birthday with champagne. We arrived at Terry's surprise dinner party about an hour late.

At the restaurant, everybody had been drinking, and they were in a fun, party mood, ready to celebrate. But instead of the 57 people we'd invited, there were only 56. Logan was absent. Actually, there were only 55 of us, because I was having an out-of-body experience. I was even more disconnected than I'd been at Rehoboth three years earlier when nobody wanted to hear what I'd learned about AIDS in San Francisco.

I'd fought depression on and off for a long time and imagined that drinking alcohol and smoking marijuana would help. They didn't. Still, I loved to drink and smoke and had done so regularly for years. The cold reality that we truly were in the midst of an unending epidemic changed everything. After visiting Logan in the hospital the night of Terry's birthday party, drinking became a desperate escape from the sadness around me. The sexual revolution of the 1960s and '70s, so liberating for so long, had come to a crashing halt. The party was over for me.

Looking back, that day marked the beginning of the end of my relationship with Terry as well. It wasn't long afterwards that Terry criticized me for being "obsessed with AIDS." He had a fair point as I became singularly focused on trying to figure out how to survive.

To his doctors' surprise, Logan survived that first hospitalization. He remained in the intensive care unit for two weeks, followed by another two months on a regular ward. During his second week in ICU, his parents came up from Florida to see him. They were a lovely, devout Methodist couple and didn't know their son was gay. He'd never told them. They arrived to find out their son was not only gay but dying. This became a common experience in the years ahead. Again and again, I saw parents come to the abrupt realization that they didn't know their sons as well they thought they did and have to learn the truth under tragic circumstances.

Together, right there in the ICU, the four of us planned Logan's memorial service. It may seem difficult to fathom now that AIDS is a treatable chronic disease, but in those early years of the epidemic, AIDS was a death sentence for almost everyone infected by the HIV virus. Logan had a lot to say about how things would go at his memorial service. He wanted it held at St. Patrick's Church, my former parish.

After visiting with Logan and his parents, I made my way home. Waiting in the mailbox was a letter from the search committee for the position of rector at St. Margaret's Church. I had been eliminated as a candidate.

Thrown back into my metaphorical wilderness, I lost all sense of direction. I recently found a passage from my journal from that time that summarized my feelings: "I am hanging in suspense, trying not to despair, looking for hope, not wanting to strike out and blame, or to scream 'What is going on!?'"

As Robert Frost said so well, "the only way out is through," and the way through such trying circumstances is to focus on what can be done in the present moment. I poured my energy into organizing Logan's friends to help him through his own wilderness. Logan hated the hospital's food, so we smuggled in carry-out meals from good restaurants to cheer him up. We also found him an AIDS buddy. When people were diagnosed with AIDS, the Whitman-Walker Clinic, a local medical center serving AIDS patients, would partner them with an AIDS buddy to provide practical and emotional support. Logan's buddy, Chip Aldridge, a student at the Wesley Theological Seminary was the best possible buddy for Logan. He was a great guy and a perfect match for Logan's temperament. Logan had the gift of gab, and Chip knew how to listen.

Our goal was to help Logan get well enough to leave the hospital. First, he had to fight off a case of pneumocystis pneumonia that could have killed him, and he did so. By the third week of November, he was released to go home.

In the beginning, only a limited number of experimental drugs and treatments were available to treat AIDS patients. AZT was the drug of choice when Logan fell ill. It didn't seem to help, and the side-effects could be debilitating. Pneumocystis pneumonia, which had attacked Logan, was one of many opportunistic diseases that could bring an AIDS patient down. AIDS compromises the immune system, so the body has difficulty fighting off illnesses that a normally healthy person would have no trouble battling. We were hearing all sorts of news out of San Francisco regarding positive results they'd had with innovative approaches. To treat pneumocystis pneumonia, they'd begun using an aerosol version of the drug Pentamidine that was inhaled directly into the lungs. Logan lived for another year after his first hospitalization. During that time, he begged and begged his doctor to start him on aerosol Pentamidine. The doctor delayed until the day before Logan died. By then it was too late.

When Terry first accused me of becoming obsessed with AIDS, I was too self-absorbed by my fears to realize the extent to which they'd overtaken me. As more and more friends sickened and died, I realized we were just beginning to feel the force of the epidemic. Many more would succumb in the years ahead, and the only questions that mattered to me were who and when and what could I do about it. In hindsight, I can see that Terry was right. I couldn't think or talk about anything else. I had become obsessed with these questions. It must have been hard for others to put up with me at times, but out of my obsession was born one of the first healing ministries for people with AIDS in the Episcopal Church.

CHAPTER FIFTEEN

CAROLE CRUMLEY

My first encounter with Episcopal healing services had taken place about six months before Logan got sick. In February of 1986, right after leaving St. Patrick's, I received a call from Carole Crumley, a priest on staff at the Washington National Cathedral. Carole was one of the first women to be ordained to the priesthood, and she and I had become close friends over the years. She'd begun conducting healing services at the Cathedral and wanted me to help.

I'd met Carole at the parish church I began attending soon after moving to Washington, Christ Church on Capitol Hill. Although I favored the ordination of women to the priesthood, there'd been no women priests in my former Diocese of Chicago. The matter was academic until I walked through the doors for my first mass at Christ Church. There stood Carole at the altar, vested in a chasuble and preparing to celebrate the Eucharist. I was entranced. The stained-glass window above the altar portrayed Jesus on the cross, with Mary and John the Beloved disciple at its foot. The inscription read, "Behold Thy Mother."

Later that year I was invited by the rector to concelebrate the Christmas Midnight Mass with him and Carole. I had never stood at the altar with a woman priest before. I could feel the difference with her next to me. I felt close to God in a way I never had before.

Ten years later, Carole was calling with an invitation to assist her with healing services she'd begun holding at 7:30 on Thursday mornings. During the communion service in the Cathedral's Bethlehem Chapel, Carole had begun the practice of laying hands on people who came forward, and praying for their healing. This was quite unusual in the Episcopal Church in those days.

When I became an Episcopal priest, the Book of Common Prayer included a service of Unction for the Sick for those requesting it. This was ordinarily done by the priest in a private setting, most often a hospital room. Those requesting the sacrament would receive the laying on of hands or be anointed with oil blessed by the bishop, and a prayer would be said for their healing. There were no public healing services, however, until the 1980s, about the time I began my AIDS ministry. Today, they happen all the time.

When I started doing public healing services, I felt that my past had caught up with me. Pentecostals are big on the laying on of hands and public healing, so it seemed that the old was becoming new for me again. In 1987, the Christian Science Monitor did a series of articles on spiritual healing. They came to the Washington National Cathedral and took a picture of Carole and me in front of the high altar with our hands on the head of someone for whom we were praying. When the photo ran in a subsequent edition of the *Monitor*, I knew any of my friends who saw it would think I'd returned to my Pentecostal holy roller roots. In a sense, perhaps I had.

My participation in those Thursday morning healing services with Carole continued for four years, and this work came to feel like a spiritual calling. I gradually realized that this was the kind of ministry where I belonged.

CHAPTER SIXTEEN

THE BISHOP WALKER VIDEO

While I was still struggling to find full-time work, yet another opportunity arose to move me past my disappointment at leaving St. Patrick's and nudge me forward in a more positive direction.

Washington's Bishop Walker had given token support for me against the Virginia Seminary's ban on supervising fieldwork students, and I felt he'd not been particularly courageous in moving the church forward on gay issues in general. Despite my feelings of ambivalence, however, I did like and respect the man for his pioneering efforts in other areas.

In the summer of 1985, Bishop Walker, who had been nominated for the office of Presiding Bishop of the Episcopal Church in the United States, was narrowly defeated by Bishop Edmund Browning. In support of Bishop Walker's nomination, I teamed up with David Lindsay, a technologically savvy young parishioner from St. Patrick's, to make a 30-minute documentary about the bishop.

We interviewed Bishop Walker's staff and shot a scene of the bishop cooking breakfast for his son. We had footage of him with Prince Charles and Princess Diana, and we included material featuring his good friend South African Bishop Desmond Tutu. It was a great disappointment to his admirers when he lost by four votes. The new Presiding Bishop, Edmond Browning, was subsequently installed in the Washington National Cathedral in an impressive, well attended service in January of 1986.

The same month as the installation of the new Presiding Bishop, the local Diocesan Convention for the Diocese of Washington took place. It was a big, two-day affair, also held in the Cathedral. At the start of the convention, David Lindsay and I put up a large screen and showed the video documentary we'd produced earlier. It was an upbeat and positive statement that affirmed Bishop Walker in his continuation as Bishop of Washington. It wasn't exactly a time of triumph for him or for me, but I felt good about contributing my creative talents on his behalf and showing I could still support my church and my bishop, regardless of my personal disappointments. There were people attending the convention who were still angry that I'd been cut loose from St. Patrick's, so the documentary served as a unifying gesture, or so I hoped.

Although I didn't belong to a particular parish at that time and felt rootless despite my part-time involvement in Carole Crumley's healing ministry, I did stay active as a priest. I blessed ten marriages in 1986 alone. In addition, I served as a supply priest, filling in for clergy who were on vacation or absent for other reasons. I celebrated weekday communion services and officiated and preached at Sunday services in churches around the diocese.

CHAPTER SEVENTEEN

New Beginnings

In October of 1986, while Logan was still in the hospital, I attended a speech given by Norman Cousins at a large Jewish synagogue. Cousins was a well-known author who promoted the healing power of laughter and positive thinking. He had written a bestseller, *Anatomy of An Illness*, about his own struggles with a life-threatening illness and awakened people to the contributions holistic medicine can make to the healing process.

There was an enormous crowd in attendance, and I found myself sitting next to John and Joan Kingdom. Joan was the Senior Warden on the vestry of St. Patrick's who'd invited me to dinner to let me know I was being fired the year before. I hadn't seen them since. John had just been diagnosed with cancer, so they were especially interested in what Norman Cousins had to say. These people who'd exercised such power over me a year before were now feeling as vulnerable as I was.

John was one of the most handsome men God ever made and a lovely human being to match. Our encounter highlighted the unpredictable nature of life. It put matters into perspective to be reminded that I was not alone in my struggles. Even those who seem above the fray are often dealing with challenges we don't imagine.

John and I formed a close bond after running into each other at the Cousins lecture, and I often visited him and Joan at their home after that. He would later prove instrumental in helping me launch my own healing ministry. While battling cancer, he managed to procure a $25,000 grant for that purpose the following year.

I would later come to regard John and others like him as

much more than mentors and fundraisers. They were angels who helped me discern the next phase of my work in the church and made it possible for me to offer pastoral care and healing to people with AIDS. These angels in human form served as earthly heralds of God's mercy and love. Many of those who suffered and died from AIDS also bore me on angels' wings as they shared their sense of God's presence and made me a better priest.

John supported me in the face of his own poor health throughout the three years remaining before his death in 1990. His wife Joan and I have remained close friends for almost 30 years.

My work with Carole's healing services at the cathedral opened my eyes and the eyes of others to new possibilities for my ministry. In the fall of 1986, my friends who ran Samaritan Ministries, Don Burnes and Alice Baum, began urging me to start an AIDS ministry. Another intuitive friend from St. Patrick's, Vicki Sant, also encouraged me to consider the possibility that I was called to such work.

I strongly resisted the call to be an AIDS chaplain. I didn't think I could bear doing AIDS work full-time. I thought it would be so depressing that I couldn't handle it. The prospect of watching promising young men dying day after day was appalling.

My friends didn't let up, despite my resistance to the opportunity God had set before me. I sometimes have to be hit over the head with a ball bat to focus my attention. Fortunately, I had friends who knew how to wield one effectively. Don and Alice continued their efforts despite my protests. Alice was a forceful woman. She'd known me for nine years by then, and she knew my soft spots. They sat me down one evening and argued persuasively that I had what it took to start an AIDS ministry. I went home afterwards in something of a daze.

The following morning, I realized with shock and trepidation that their arguments had taken hold. After weeks of ignoring the obvious, it was at last clear what I had to do. I was born under the sign of Aries the Ram. We can be stubborn, but once we come to a decision, we commit quickly and fully. "Perhaps this is why I did thirteen quarters of clinical pastoral education at Rush-Presbyterian-St. Luke's Medical Center back in Chicago in the

'70s," I thought to myself. Colleagues had questioned my sanity for having endured such intense chaplaincy training, but now I would put it to the test.

I had no idea how an AIDS ministry would be funded, but the first thing I did was phone Bishop Walker's secretary and ask for an appointment. I wanted the bishop's blessing for what I knew would be a monumental undertaking. A week later, I entered his office right next to the cathedral with some trepidation. To my relief and delight, he told me he thought outreach to the AIDS community was a good idea. He sent me to see Sanford Garner, rector of one of the well-established WASP churches in the diocese, Christ Church in Georgetown. Among Sanford's parishioners were George and Barbara Bush.

Sanford was in a position to help. Unbeknownst to me, the son of two members of his congregation, Peter and Melody Gilsey, had recently died from AIDS. Sanford was a southerner and a proper, traditionalist member of the clergy. He was also a man of compassion and action. After seeing what the Gilseys had endured when their son died, he had asked neighboring Episcopal parishes to send representatives to a meeting to discuss what they could do about the AIDS epidemic. Sixteen parishes had responded, and in record time they raised $30,000 and formed a committee to administer the fund.

Seeking an effective way to put these funds to work, the committee had entered into discussions with the Whitman-Walker Clinic, the largest gay medical center in Washington, D.C. The clinic was named after the iconic gay writer Walt Whitman and Dr. Mary Walker, a woman doctor who wore men's clothing and was awarded the Medal of Honor for her brave service during the Civil War. The clinic was a first responder to the AIDS epidemic in the D.C. area and a leader in its diagnosis and treatment.

The committee decided that the $30,000 raised by the local Episcopal churches would be used to fund a housing facility for men living with AIDS, the Michael Haas Residence, named after an Episcopal organist who had died a few years before.

Terry and I had attended Michael Haas's funeral with Terry's parents at St. Paul's Church on K Street, and I remember feeling very uncomfortable with them during the service. AIDS was new on the scene, and people still didn't know how it was transmitted. Now, just a few years later, the first residence to house men with

AIDS was being named in Michael's memory.

I met with Sanford Garner soon after being referred by Bishop Walker, and he sent me to meet with April Hockett, a socially conscious laywoman who'd been named chair of the committee formed to administer the funds raised by local parishes to help people suffering with AIDS. Following an initial meeting, April and I brought in a few other concerned laypeople over the next few months to discuss further fundraising efforts and projects. We reached an agreement early on that we wanted to start a nonprofit AIDS organization with me as its chaplain.

The committee named this organization the Episcopal Caring Response to AIDS, Inc., which became popularly known as ECRA. It was a big deal for the acronym "AIDS" to be included in the title because of the widespread paranoia that surrounded the disease. But we wanted it in the title, just as we wanted "Episcopal" in there to show the church's involvement and commitment.

That fall of 1986, I completed a training course at the Whitman-Walker Clinic to educate myself medically about AIDS. I also became a member of a newly formed Diocesan AIDS Commission organized by Kwasi Thornell, a canon at the National Cathedral.

Soon after the Haas House was established, Bob Alfandre, a gay entrepreneur and philanthropist on the Board of the Whitman-Walker Clinic, donated money to open a second residence for men with AIDS. It was a bungalow named the Carroll Sledz House in honor of his lover who had died earlier that year.

The opening of the Sledz House was well-timed to receive our friend Logan Sallada, who was desperate to get well and out of the hospital. We were able to spring Logan from the hospital that November and procured a room for him at the Sledz House, where he joined four other men in residence.

It took us about three hours to complete the paperwork for Logan's hospital release, and once we were in the car, he said, "Can we just drive around Washington for a little while? I've so missed seeing the city." We had that in common; we both loved the place. We circled the Capitol building and then drove along the north side of the National Mall past the Washington Monument and up around the White House. Then he said, "Let's go by the Willard Hotel." The Willard Hotel had been undergoing a major restoration. President Lincoln had stayed there just prior to his inauguration, so the building had a distinguished history. From there we drove on to the Lincoln and Jefferson memorials before finally heading to Logan's new home.

I'd been keen to get Logan settled into the Sledz House and was glad he was taking such a strong interest in his surroundings; it seemed like a good sign. We were lucky that the new AIDS residence had opened in time to take Logan in when he had nowhere else to turn.

Logan's illness radically changed his world view. He'd been an outspoken Republican, but his AIDS diagnosis turned him into a social democrat. He was now dependent on social services to survive and realized he'd be destitute and homeless without them.

Logan's move from the hospital to the Sledz residence was fraught with anxiety. He'd been near death, and the improvement in his health meant he had to adjust to starting over. He was certainly not out of the woods, but he'd gone from zero to 100 mph in a short period of time. In the months ahead, he would swing back and forth.

Shortly after New Year's, Terry and I flew Logan down to Key West. I'd never been there, but Logan had visited the area many times and had even met the playwright and author Tennessee Williams, who had a house there. Logan later gave me one of Tennessee's books, signed by the author.

After visiting Key West, we planned to fly to Florida's west coast to see Logan's parents for a few days. Logan brought along a chandelier that had been dismantled and wrapped in a canvas carry-on bag as a gift for his mother. On the final leg of our flight, we boarded a small commuter plane to take us to Key West from Miami. The chandelier bag wouldn't fit in the luggage compartment, so I volunteered to nurse it aboard the plane.

Just as we settled in, Logan turned around from the seat in front of me and began telling me how to hold the bag properly so as not to cause any damage. Losing patience with the whole thing, I blurted, "Yes Logan! I've got the damn chandelier in hand. Stop telling me what to do!"

I regretted my words as soon as they left my mouth. It was the fragility of Logan's life, not the chandelier, we were worried about. My angry words were just a mask for the anxiety I felt about him and about the challenges that lay ahead.

We had a lovely time relaxing and enjoying the atmosphere in Key West. Afterwards, Terry and I spent a few days with Logan and his parents at their home on the Gulf of Mexico before heading back to Washington. Logan stayed on to have a little more time alone with his folks, but he was eager to join us at home. He'd bought tickets to take us to see Les Miserables at the Kennedy Center and was excited about seeing the musical together.

I needed the money so was delighted when the Diocesan Employment Office recommended me for a part-time job as the interim priest at St. Monica's, a small African American parish on Capitol Hill not far from where we'd lived when we first moved to Washington. I began serving in that position in January of 1987.

One week later, the parish's recently divorced former rector died of AIDS-related complications. Although the cause of his death was an open secret, the word "AIDS" was never mentioned. His funeral was well-attended, and Bishop Walker presided at the service. I was the only white person in the congregation.

The congregation knew I was only temporary and that my focus was on planning meetings and raising money for the fledgling Episcopal Caring Response to AIDS. As parishioners learned more about those other activities, they became increasingly comfortable talking about AIDS and coming to terms with the death of their former rector.

I served at St. Monica's for six months. I was there through Lent and Holy Week and celebrated the Resurrection of our Lord with them on Easter Sunday. As the only priest on staff, I found it draining but deeply satisfying. When my time was up, I returned home to my gardening and devoted more of my energy to my ECRA work.

I'd become close friends with Logan's AIDS buddy, Chip Aldridge, who was studying to be a Methodist minister at Wesley Theological Seminary in Washington. In February of 1987 we designed a one-day conference on AIDS to be held at his seminary. Among others, we invited Dr. Anthony Fauci to participate in a panel discussion at the conference. Dr. Fauci was a young, up-and-coming medical researcher who headed the AIDS Research Center at the National Institute of Health. National Public Radio talk show host Diane Rehm agreed to be the moderator, and we flew in Bill Barcus, an openly gay priest from San Francisco, to round out the panel.

I'd met Bill in the 1970s when he was in seminary. Hailing from Wichita, Kansas, Bill was one of the brightest, most articulate speakers we could hope for. He was also one of the funniest, gutsiest human beings I'd ever met. When he'd first talked to the bishop of Kansas about going to seminary, the bishop refused to support him because Bill was gay. However, Bishop Montgomery of Chicago, who had ordained me, took him in.

Fast-forward to 1979 when Bill was a priest at San Francisco's St. Mary's Episcopal Church, one of the city's more well-to-do parishes. I'd read in The New York Times that he'd come out as gay while preaching a sermon at St. Mary's. This was unheard of in those days and took more courage than most of us could imagine. Eloquent and proud as he espoused the full humanity of homosexual persons, Bill was a guide and mentor for thousands, a brave and inspiring role model. His example had strengthened my own resolve to live an authentic life as an openly gay man within my priesthood.

When I learned that Bill had been appointed to head the Episcopal Church's AIDS ministry in San Francisco and that he himself had AIDS, I realized he'd be a perfect candidate to take part in the AIDS conference I was setting up with Chip Aldridge. Bill agreed to be our keynote speaker, and he lit a fire under everyone present. The conference was a great success.

Following the conference, Bill and I were interviewed by Diane Rehm on her highly regarded NPR talk show. I'd met Diane at St. Patrick's in late 1979 when I filled in briefly before Jim Steen arrived as their new rector. Her star was just beginning to rise as a radio personality. She was one of the laypeople licensed by the bishop to assist the priest with the communion service. After the service, Diane had invited me to join her and her husband, John, for brunch. Later, in 1981, she was on the St. Patrick's vestry that voted me in as their assistant rector.

Diane's talk show ran for two hours, and Bill and I were featured for an hour of that time. People phoned in, and we talked about the AIDS epidemic. Bill had an infectious sense of humor, and I had to avoid looking at him because he could make me laugh with the blink of an eye.

Bill had AIDS, and I was on guard not to become infected myself. Friends were dying on every side. We had every right to feel gloomy, but Bill always knew how to keep up his own and everyone else's spirits. Before we faced the microphones in Diane's studio, I insisted we settle down. He had quipped to me, "Dearie, if you keep your good looks and my health holds out, we'll be bishops yet." "Bill," I said to him, "we've got to stop laughing. We can't go on the air laughing when we talk about AIDS!" We tacitly agreed not to look at each other until the show was over.

The Diane Rehm Show was a godsend. It boosted our spirits and brought our work to the attention of thousands who would otherwise have been unaware of our ministry to the AIDS community. Listeners called in with offers of financial and volunteer support. Working with Diane was a deeply bonding experience and further strengthened our friendship.

Blessings continued to fall on our nascent organization. Late on Good Friday afternoon as I toiled in my garden, Bill called from California and exclaimed, "You've got to meet Meg Graham. She's a gold mine! She will find you money!" A successful, middle-aged professional woman, Meg was in seminary and was also working with Common Cause, a "good government" watchdog group based in D.C. Meg advised me on raising money for ECRA, and her contributions were key to our progress as the ministry gained momentum. Meg became another one of the angels who came into my life and made the ministry work.

Meanwhile, there was still a lot of nonsense getting in the way of rational discussion about AIDS, both in the church and the nation as a whole. The Diocese of Washington remained part of the Old South in some respects due to its geographical location. When I visited its parishes to talk to their congregations about AIDS, I sometimes heard the term "sodomite" whispered in the audience. There were calls to quarantine people with AIDS, hardly in accord with the example set by Jesus in his healing of the blind, the lame, and those afflicted with leprosy.

The quarantine movement was given considerable momentum by Bible-thumping preachers across the land who proclaimed that AIDS was God's punishment for sin. They didn't argue the same for arthritis or heart disease. The Reagan administration remained silent, so there was no help coming from that quarter. After my friend Logan got sick, I encouraged him to call his former boss, Cabinet Secretary Elizabeth Dole, and tell her he had AIDS. Logan had served as Dole's Executive Assistant when she headed up the Transportation Department.

"You need to light a fire under them," I insisted. "Make it personal for them." Logan would only sigh and reply, "You don't understand. AIDS is not on the Reagan administration's agenda. They don't want to hear about it." A few weeks would go by, and I'd reapply the pressure: "Logan, call Elizabeth Dole!" Living in Washington where the Reagans were so visible and their silence so deafening became an exercise in frustration. We were swimming against the tide.

I was on the Diane Rehm show again that year, and the second time she interviewed me with Logan. Logan used his bar name, "Rob," throughout the interview. He still wasn't ready to come out to the world at large, a measure of the shame associated with being gay and having AIDS in those years. It was brave of him to participate at all, but he knew the show gave my budding AIDS ministry invaluable exposure, and he wanted to help.

CHAPTER EIGHTEEN

Breaking the Silence

The customary silence about sexual orientation and cause of death at funerals and memorial services for gay men who died of AIDS didn't last. Change came about because the gay community would no longer put up with anything but the truth. After watching their friends and loved ones die with dignity and courage under often terrible conditions, the survivors decided they weren't about to dishonor their memories by lying about them.

There was another aspect to these services that became clear over time. Gay couples couldn't legally marry, so we'd never been able to celebrate our unions in the way heterosexual couples could. That changed as AIDS began to decimate our community. Services celebrating the lives of those who had died of AIDS began to celebrate their relationships with longtime companions as well. At funerals and memorial services across the country, we lifted up the lives not only of those who had died but of the significant others who loved them. We blessed these loving unions at their end rather than at their beginning.

Those who were left behind realized that their silence had contributed to the national state of denial about AIDS and the government's unwillingness to fund research for effective treatments. Gay activist groups had sprung up in New York and elsewhere demanding action from the federal government and pushing for greater funding to search for a cure. One particularly active group, the AIDS Coalition to Unleash Power—better known as ACT UP—carried a banner that became iconic: Silence = Death. For too long, their voices went unheard. The Reagan administration continued its silence as thousands perished.

I was determined not to be complicit in the silence. Early

in 1987, I was called to the hospital to see a young man who had AIDS. He was a handsome, blonde, blue-eyed 24-year-old. He didn't look particularly ill, but he was. His parents, who were visiting him with their Lutheran minister, were polite but reserved. What struck me about the setting was that no one touched the young man, not even the minister when he prayed for him. Whenever I prayed one-on-one with someone in a hospital room, I would anoint them with oil and gently place my hands on their head.

Several months later, I attended the young man's funeral in Northern Virginia. An Episcopal priest who had befriended him stood to tell the congregation about his experience of knowing the young man and mentioned that he was gay. Afterwards, when he and I spoke, I expressed surprise at what he'd done because the family had been so closeted about their son. He replied, "I didn't give them the opportunity to say no."

It struck me then and there that the young man had wanted people to know he was gay. He'd been struggling to find himself and was just beginning to come out as a gay man when he fell sick. This was becoming a familiar pattern. Young men on the threshold of claiming authenticity in their lives would die of AIDS and be shoved back into the closet by their grieving families.

After what I witnessed at this funeral, I thought to myself, "I'm going to do the same thing." If the person who was dying wanted to be out, I was going to honor their wishes regardless of what the family wanted.

CHAPTER NINETEEN

LAUNCHING THE EPISCOPAL CARING RESPONSE TO AIDS

I completed my work at St. Monica's in June of 1987, the same month ECRA was formally incorporated as a nonprofit organization. The signing of the official documents took place in the office of a young lawyer by the name of Trevor Potter. Trevor was a gay Episcopal layman who had become our pro bono legal counsel. April Hockett and I signed the documents along with another gay layman, Eric Scharf.

Trevor became another of my angels. I doubt I'd have made it through all the political machinations surrounding my AIDS ministry if he hadn't been there as a steadying presence and wise counselor. He had sandy blonde hair and rosy cheeks. He was the exact opposite of the kind of man I was usually attracted to, but I developed a crush on him all the same—a crush that remains to this day.

Trevor was from an aristocratic Chicago family and looked every inch a Republican, which he was. A graduate of Harvard, he was the quintessential opposite of this hayseed from Herrin at the other end of Illinois from Chicago. Despite his privileged background, Trevor was utterly lacking in pretense. He was straightforward with an open and honest Midwestern charm. Later, President George H. W. Bush appointed him to chair the Federal Election Commission. He's now a leading authority on federal election law.

We made a serious mistake when we incorporated ECRA, but we didn't know it at the time. We were inexperienced and naïve in the way we structured the board when we wrote the by-laws. Flying high on the positive responses we'd received from the sixteen Episcopal parishes that helped fund us, we stipulated that each of those parishes could send two representatives to sit on the board. That meant a board of at least thirty-two people. If you've ever sat on a board or committee, you know that it can be difficult enough to get three people to agree on something, let alone dozens.

As new parishes contributed funds and joined the organization, they, too, were entitled to send two parishioners to represent them on the board. Eventually, the board had seventy-four members. About a year into our ministry, we realized we needed an executive committee that would meet monthly to handle routine business, while the board met quarterly to address more significant policy issues.

The executive committee was comprised of eighteen members who ran the organization by majority vote without an executive director. Alas, that was still too many people to administer the organization efficiently. I was just the chaplain responsible for pastoral work and had no administrative authority of my own.

April Hockett was chair for the first year, and things went well. As long as we had good leadership, the organization held together, and we were okay. We were navigating turbulent waters and faced considerable prejudice from powerful quarters. We needed a deft pilot at the wheel. Unfortunately, we lost that for a while when April moved on.

While the enthusiasm of the incoming board members was initially encouraging, we soon found ourselves with too many hands on deck. The second year became increasingly difficult as the consequences of our mistake in structuring the organization caught up with us. Finally, Trevor stepped in and organized a slate of officers that set things straight. They elected a new chair, Steve Lembesis, who guided our work wisely and well for the next four years. I came to rely on Steve and to love him deeply. He, too, became one of my angels.

CHAPTER TWENTY

ANGELS

The title of my memoir, "Ordained by Angels" refers to the fact that my AIDS ministry would not have been possible—indeed, my life would not have been possible—without the help of angels in human and spirit form. They gave of their time and money throughout my ministry, and their love and support healed lives and guided my spiritual path. This memoir is dedicated, in large part, to them.

One of the first angels to bless my ministry was Vicky Sant. Vicky was an intuitive and quietly effective layperson at St. Patrick's who recognized the need for an AIDS chaplaincy early in the epidemic. I'd met Vicki in 1979 and felt a strong connection with her from the beginning. Vicki's gentle nature was coupled with tough-minded administrative skills that served her well as a board member and chair of several major charities.

In the spring of 1987, Vicki hosted a breakfast meeting to strategize on fundraising activities to raise money for our AIDS ministry. Afterwards, she said to me, "Jerry, you need to find somebody who's been personally touched by AIDS to help you raise money." She realized that without personal involvement, it was all too easy for people to turn a blind eye.

Someone at the breakfast had mentioned that they had friends, Peter and Melody Gilsey, whose son had died of AIDS early the previous year. This was the couple whose tragic loss had inspired the rector of Christ Church in Georgetown to work with neighboring parishes and raise the $30,000 that was used to fund the Michael Haas residence for men living with AIDS. The Gilseys, too, would join the company of angels who sustained our ministry through the years.

I was introduced to the Gilseys, and the three of us had lunch. Peter, a middle-aged stockbroker from an East Coast blue-blood Episcopal family, could seem staid, but that was just a front. His glamorous younger wife, Melody, was a fashion plate. The TV series, Dallas, was popular then, and she would have fit right in. The choir at Christ Church in Georgetown loved it when she approached the altar wearing her latest outfit. Melody was an exuberant extrovert who became one of our leading champions over the next several years.

Melody was an outstanding fundraiser. She threw galas and balls and staged other events to raise money for worthy causes. One day she confided, "Before he died, I promised my son, David, that I would raise money for AIDS."

Peter was busily involved with a number of social service activities around town. He befriended residents with AIDS at the Sledz House, which was not far from where the Gilseys lived. He would visit and have meals with them and help them out financially. He did it quietly and without fuss. Few people knew the depth of his generosity and compassion.

I grew to love Melody and Peter. As people like the Gilseys got involved in the ministry, I felt increasingly empowered and confident of its success. None of it happened overnight, though, and there was never universal agreement about the urgency of the AIDS epidemic. Melody relied on the help of a group of women to organize events, and it was a challenge to convince them to take up our cause. "I have to convince the committee of the ladies I work with that we can do this," she told me. "They're kind but reluctant." It took two years before she was able to organize a gala that helped put us on a firm financial footing.

On June 16, 1987, we held a service in the Bishop's Chapel adjacent to the National Cathedral to inaugurate and bless our new AIDS ministry. Assistant Bishop Ron Haines led the service, and Logan was there. I thought of Logan as my patron saint. Once we got over the shock that I wasn't going to be rector at St. Margaret's, he rallied and resumed his position as my chief cheerleader. Nearly 60 people attended the service, mostly board members and clergy.

Following the service in the Bishop's Chapel, we adjourned for a lovely reception in the nearby Bishop's Garden. With that, the Episcopal Caring Response to AIDS was officially launched, and I was its chaplain. I received a part-time salary and worked out of my office from home in Virginia. I continued to drive to the cathedral for healing services with Carole Crumley every Thursday morning. My new ministry had formally begun.

CHAPTER TWENTY-ONE

THREE STORIES OF COURAGE AND HEALING

I was raised on stories about courage and healing handed down by my parents and grandparents. These family tales were a source of comfort and encouragement throughout the years of my AIDS ministry. They got me through some very tough times.

Hospital chaplaincy is not for everyone. Priests, like anyone else, can be squeamish and fearful around serious illness. I knew clergy who refused to visit parishioners with AIDS at home or in the hospital before they died. Too many young men with AIDS died alone, abandoned by their families and friends who were terrified of the disease. On some level, they couldn't help but think, "Maybe I'm next." And sometimes they were.

I was not immune to such fears. I was scared witless when first confronted by friends dying of AIDS. I couldn't imagine a more terrible way to die. AIDS threatened to rob the sufferer of all dignity. Contracting AIDS meant that your life was torn open for all to see.

I'd had extensive chaplaincy training in a hospital setting, but none of it fully prepared me for the specter that faced us as the plague took hold: years of suffering and death with no end in sight. As I contemplated life as an AIDS chaplain, the courage exemplified by my ancestors as they faced the challenges of their own time inspired me to go forward and carried me through the subsequent years of death and despair.

The stories we hear about our families as children, repeatedly told, often take on mythological proportions. Along with photo albums and scrapbooks, they forever shape the images we keep of ourselves and our roots.

Throughout childhood, my siblings and I heard what I called the "Big Three" stories that formed the basis of our family folklore. We heard them over and over again as our elders wove fact and legend into powerful lessons. These stories mark the psychological and spiritual foundations upon which I was able to build a healing ministry with AIDS patients much later in life. The "Big Three" stories were supplemented by various other tales that fleshed out my impressions of family members who'd gone before me.

The first of the "Big Three" stories was told by my great-aunt Hattie who lived to be 101 years old and was like a grandmother to us. Her tale was set in 1904 and involved the Luckeys, my father's deeply religions grandparents, whose parents had migrated to Tennessee to settle in the frontier county of Williamson before the Civil War. Hattie's father, Marshall Luckey, was a small businessman who opened a café and a shoe store just after the turn of the century in the newly established town of Herrin where I was born many years later

When Aunt Hattie was 12 years old, a stranger came into Marshall's café late one afternoon perspiring profusely and asking for water. Marshall gave him water and thought no more about it until the next day when the man was found dead in an alleyway. He'd died of smallpox.

Although the incidence of smallpox had diminished considerably by that time thanks to vaccination, untreated cases were often deadly. During his brief encounter with the man from out of town, Marshall was infected. He soon fell sick with a high fever and pustular rash. To keep the disease from spreading, Hattie's three brothers took their father out of the house in the middle of the night and carried him in a buggy to the "pest house" on the outskirts of town. The "pest house" was a place where people with dangerous communicable diseases could be placed in quarantine to protect the general population.

All of the members of the family were inoculated against smallpox, but only Marshall was quarantined. Even though smallpox was highly contagious, Ruth visited the pest house every day, bringing meals and comfort to her husband. She loved her husband and her children, and she simply did what she had to do to take care of them.

Marshall died despite Ruth's efforts, but her sons survived.

The story of her courage in the presence of a highly infectious disease made a lasting impression on me. Her example encouraged me at times when I was anxious and afraid. She joined me in spirit as I visited people with AIDS before it was fully understood how one caught the virus. I knew I was doing the right thing because my great-grandmother had done the right thing before me. She was my inspiration.

As is common in family mythology, one story blurs into the next, and not all of them involved courage or healing. As a footnote to this story, after Marshall died, Ruth married a Baptist preacher, the Reverend John Banks. Grieving the loss of their father, Aunt Hattie and her siblings hated Reverend Banks. "He was a phony," she told me. "When we had company for dinner, he would pray long, pious prayers, but when nobody was visiting, he wouldn't bother." Throughout my ministry in Washington D.C., I heard Hattie's voice: "Don't be a phony." I hear it to this day.

There was precedent in my family for my own later experiences with death and dying. My father was no stranger to death. In 1917, when he was a teenager, Dad lost his older brother, Ralph Waldo, in a tragic shooting accident. Ralph was a handsome, popular young man who was engaged to be married to a doctor's daughter, quite a step up for our family. The tragedy occurred when Dad and Ralph went hunting with some other guys, and the group decided to take a break. Ralph leaned back on a split-rail fence and set the butt of the rifle on the ground, resting the barrel between his legs. The fence broke, Ralph slipped, and the gun, still cocked, fired and shot him through the heart. We rarely spoke of this, but years later, Dad named his first son Ralph Waldo after his brother. My brother's death, only eight days after he was born, also left a quiet but lasting impact.

On one of my visits back home in the 1970s, Dad and I drove up to see Dad's sister, Maude. I adored Aunt Maude. She and Dad were elderly by that time, and somehow my late Uncle Ralph came up in conversation. I just listened. I'd been a priest for quite a while by then and knew to listen without interruption when others talked about death. It was immediately apparent how much Dad and his sister were grieving the loss of their brother more than fifty years later. I realized anew that my father and I had both lost brothers. While I mourned the loss of Ralph

Waldo after the fact, Dad was mourning the loss of both his brother and his son, neither of whom I'd ever actually met.

The death of Dad's brother was the second death he experienced in a short period of time. His father had died just the year before of colon cancer at the age of 42. These untimely deaths, within a year of each other, led to significant changes in Dad's life. Dad had to quit high school at age 16 and go to work in the coal mines to help support the family. His mother, Myrtle, was in her thirties and was left with seven children to feed. Uncle Booster later told me that Grandma Myrtle had thrown herself on the ground in the cornfield and cried out to God, "Why have you done this to me?"

The second of the "Big Three" family stories that inspired my ministry, and probably the one with the greatest ripple effect, featured Dad's mother, my Grandma Myrtle Anderson. After her husband and eldest son died within a year and with seven children to support, she went to work in a local greenhouse. While cutting plants one day, she sliced her finger and developed an infection that turned into blood poisoning. Her doctor thought he might have to amputate, but Myrtle had other plans. A Pentecostal evangelist was holding a healing revival out on the edge of town. In those days they didn't use tents but took branches from trees and put up posts to build a "brush arbor," a crude structure to house public gatherings outdoors. My father drove his mother to the revival site in the horse and buggy but made her walk the last two blocks. He didn't want anybody to see him associating with those holy rollers.

Her son's skeptical disdain aside, Grandma Myrtle had a great revival. She was baptized in the Holy Ghost, and she spoke in tongues. Her blood poisoning was healed. She returned to the Baptist Church, but she refused to stop speaking in tongues. She ignored the Baptist minister's orders to cease and desist, so he finally wrote her a letter of excommunication.

That didn't slow Grandma Myrtle down one bit. She became one of the founding members of the First Pentecostal Church in Herrin, and that church exists today. All but one of Myrtle's kids became Pentecostal, and two of them—my dad and Uncle Booster—became ministers. So did yours truly, her grandson, although in a different tradition. I grew up with Grandma Myrtle's example set firmly before me: She was healed by the purity and conviction of her faith.

These early stories were powerful and compelling, but they were set in a time before I was born. They felt like folklore. The third of the "Big Three" family stories tells of my father's brush with death, and it took place during my lifetime.

Work in the coal mines was hard and dangerous. In some of the mines, Dad worked crouching over and standing in water for hours on end. He worked especially long shifts during World War II when demand for coal skyrocketed. This was probably when he contracted tuberculosis. When the disease was diagnosed some time later, he was isolated from the family for several months. Later he told us that in the depths of his illness, Jesus had come to him and stood at the end of his bed. "I am going to heal you, and you are going to live to see your two small children grow into adulthood" Jesus said. Dad returned to us in record time, fully recovered.

From that time on, I watched my father testify before our Pentecostal congregation about his miraculous vision and healing. Pentecostals are big on healing and even bigger on testifying. People regularly testified as to how God had healed them or saved them from alcohol or tobacco or whatever else had troubled their bodies and souls. This was before 12-step programs. Pentecostals would just pour it all out. Not surprisingly, I used to think, "My God, I'd be an orphan if this healing hadn't happened."

These stories left an indelible mark on me as a young boy trying to find his place in his family and in his world. They carried transforming power for my elders, and this rubbed off on me. They gave evidence of God's healing presence and power in the lives of my parents, grandparents, and great-grandparents, decade after decade, generation after generation. These family stories dealt with issues of love and life and death and the power of healing through sheer purity of belief. My ancestors' tales were with me through all the years of my AIDS ministry. I hadn't fully appreciated the power of their stories until I found myself in the middle of the AIDS crisis and drew them into myself.

If I'd been hired as rector at St. Margaret's, I'd probably never have found the fulfillment I did through my work as an AIDS chaplain. I've never forgotten Carole Crumley's characteristically upbeat and positive response when I told her I'd been turned down by St. Margaret's: "You know, Jerry, maybe God has something in store for you that's bigger than the boundaries of St. Margaret's parish." I couldn't imagine what that might be, but her intuition was correct. Two months after my AIDS ministry began, St. Margaret's was one of the sixteen churches that donated money and sent representatives to our board. I came to realize I was much happier exercising the flexibility and freedom of pastoral ministry than being tied down by the institutional constraints of serving in a parish.

CHAPTER TWENTY-TWO

LOGAN, DEBBIE, AND NICK

In July of 1987, Terry and I and a couple of friends decided to take Logan Sallada to the beach. Logan had been in and out of the hospital a few more times with pneumonia, so his energy was limited. Still, he was able to socialize by going out to dinner and the movies with friends. We all liked to think that he was somehow going to make it, that he wasn't going to die.

We'd rented a house at Rehoboth right on the water with a lovely view. Terry and I hadn't been back to Rehoboth since that disturbing stay in 1983, when I'd felt so isolated after my trip to San Francisco. Terry drove up separately with our friends, and I made the three-hour trip with Logan as my navigator. It was good to be with my friend, but it didn't feel like a festive occasion. We knew we'd not be dressing up to go to a gay bar or hanging out at the beach. Our mood was subdued.

The drive through the countryside put Logan in a philosophical mood. He remained silent for a while, taking in the scenery, but then pointed ahead. "That tree," he said. "It's dead. And it's standing there all by itself." I couldn't help thinking, "That tree is Logan." We didn't discuss it any further, but he obviously felt the nearness of death. It had been his companion for many months.

Not long before our trip to Rehoboth, I was approached by a therapist named Nancy Shands who was seeking to interview people with AIDS as part of a book she was writing. I referred her to Logan, and he agreed to be interviewed.

The book, *AIDS: The Lonely Voyage*, came out in 1988, shortly after Logan died. Nancy later told me that she'd taken the title from Logan's reference to his experience of living with AIDS as a lonely voyage. Initially, I felt deeply wounded. We had done so much for Logan. We'd tried so hard. I'd poured myself into the support group we formed for him; yet, he still felt lonely.

Other caregivers have had similar experiences. No matter how diligently we try to help and comfort those in our care, we can accompany them only so far on their journeys. I've come to accept that they have to take long stretches of their voyages alone. Perhaps that's what Logan was trying to tell me on that drive to Rehoboth.

A month after our trip to the beach, Terry and I took Logan to visit Terry's parents' modest thirteen acre farm at the foot of the Blue Ridge Mountains. The farm had served as a refuge for family and friends for years. Three of my angels from Washington joined us there: Dora Richardson, Dr. Fred Morgan, and his wife Carlin Rankin. Dora was a wealthy parishioner I'd known from my years at St. Patrick's and had become an active supporter of our AIDS ministry. Her family were liberal southern Democrats from way back who had often given to worthy causes. Fred was the first doctor I'd ever talked to about AIDS, back in 1982. He and Carlin were unfailingly supportive of my AIDS ministry.

The six of us had dinner at the nearby Inn at Little Washington, renowned for its culinary excellence. Logan was enraptured. Terry and I joked with Logan that if he died while in rural Virginia, we'd put him in the trunk of the car and take him back to the city. Out there in the country, they'd have gone berserk over someone with AIDS. We shared a macabre sense of humor.

I'd borrowed a little sports car from my friend Robin Deck, and at the end of our visit Logan and I took a drive up into the Blue Ridge mountain highlands where it's especially beautiful. Logan was passionate about two things: refugee Tibetan monks he'd met in India when he worked in the Peace Corps and the environment. He'd been the youngest member of the United States delegation to the first international environmental conference in Stockholm in 1972, and he'd taken his role seriously. As we reached the summit, Logan asked that we stop the car. "See how the foliage at the top of the trees is thin and not so verdant? That's because of industrial pollution coming across from Ohio and the Midwest," he explained. Logan was the first person to raise my awareness of the ravages of environmental pollution and the dangers it posed to our planet. As his own death approached, Logan's concern for—and identification with—environmental decay made a lasting impression on me.

That August, I met a woman with AIDS for the first time. Her name was Debbie. She called me on the phone one day and asked me to come and see her out in Maryland, about half an hour away. There was something odd about the way she spoke, but I couldn't put my finger on it. She told me where she lived, that her husband would be at work, that the front door would be open, and that she might be in her bedroom. Hmmm. I called Jean Rogers, a parishioner I'd known at St. Patrick's who was now in seminary. I'd performed her wedding, so she knew me quite well. I explained the situation and asked if she'd accompany me. Jean agreed and off we went.

Just as Debbie had said, the front door was open, and she was in bed. Debbie had AIDS-related dementia. She showed us pictures of herself and her husband. They were both musicians. Once a beautiful woman, she was now gaunt and struggling for life. As we talked, she gradually regressed to a childlike state and sounded more and more like an irrepressibly sweet little girl. It was clear she shouldn't be left alone, and she was soon placed in a hospice run by Mother Theresa's ascetic order of nuns. Debbie died in November of 1988. Her husband asked me to conduct the burial service at the cemetery, and I did so.

Around the same time, I got another call asking for a pastoral visit from a man named Nick. In his early forties, Nick was from a family of well-established Washington bankers. They'd founded an important newspaper a hundred years earlier and were Episcopalians. Nick was a closeted gay man with AIDS. He was single and had no gay friends.

Bob Alfandre, the angel who'd funded the Carroll Sledz House where Logan was living, owned a magnificent house in Washington. When Bob threw a swim party for the guys from the Sledz House and a few others with AIDS, I took Nick. Nick had never been to a party of just gay men, and he had a delightful time. It thrilled his family to see him so happy. We were making progress in our efforts to make the lives of people with AIDS at least a little bit better.

In the fall of 1987, a group of us went to see Charles Perry, the provost and administrative head of the Washington National Cathedral. We knew he was homophobic, but other cathedrals in places like New York City and San Francisco had already offered public statements of support by designating altars or other special areas where people could go to pray and light candles for those suffering with AIDS. We wanted to do something similar in Washington. Sadly, it was like talking to a wall, and I left feeling discouraged by the provost's utter lack of receptivity.

On September 25, 1987, Logan was readmitted to George Washington Hospital. He'd been unable to shake the pneumocystis pneumonia that had been haunting him for the past year. He wasn't doing well. I visited him almost every day. I held his medical power of attorney, which stated that Logan did not want to be sustained on respirators or other life support. I saw him on the evening of October 6th, after he'd just received his first dose of aerosolized Pentamidine, a new treatment that offered a level of hope. I brought some soup that Terry had made at home, but Logan's throat was too sore to eat anything. He was exhausted, so I didn't stay long.

Late that evening, while I was sitting in my small home office with its view of the Capitol dome across the Potomac River, a magnificent thunderstorm swept through, illuminating the darkness with flashes of lightning. In the middle of the storm, Logan's doctor called. It was around 9:30p.m., and he said, "I think we need to put Logan on a respirator. His lungs are collapsing, but I need your permission." I explained Logan's wishes, to which he replied, "I know, but when I mentioned this possibility to him earlier he gave me the go-ahead." I asked how long they would keep him on it. "No more than four days," he replied. I gave my assent, then hung up the phone and cried.

The next day, the hospital called and left several messages on my answering machine saying that the respirator wasn't working for Logan. They wanted me to come in and sign the necessary papers to remove it. The first message was left at noon, but I didn't get any of them until later that afternoon when I returned to my office. When the hospital had first called, I was giving communion to James, a young man with AIDS, at his apartment. During the communion, I'd felt a chill and thought I heard a swooshing sound and briefly wondered if Logan had died. I asked James if he had also heard or felt what I had experienced. He said maybe it was a spirit visiting. Since I was taking James out to lunch in his wheelchair, I didn't find out the hospital was trying to reach me until later.

Like me, Logan was an Aires. Having been born just two days after me in the same year, he was an impulsive and determined decision maker. When I finally heard the messages from the hospital, I fantasized that Logan had been pressuring them from beyond the veil of consciousness to get my permission to turn off the respirator. He wanted to be rid of it. I hurried to the hospital and signed the papers. After they removed the respirator, I called several friends, who came and gathered around Logan's bed. At one point there were eight of us. One was a Franciscan brother who had been Logan's much-loved caregiver. His AIDS buddy Chip Aldridge and longtime benefactor Peter Gilsey were also there. Logan died quietly at 1:15a.m. on October 8th without drama or struggle.

The next Sunday, I was scheduled to preach a sermon at Grace Church in Georgetown. Grace was a progressive, liberal Episcopal parish. During the Nixon era, they had a hippie priest who turned the church into a theater and housed political protestors against the war in Vietnam. They had also provided office space to the Whitman-Walker Clinic when it first started out as a gay VD clinic. Normally, I'd have been glad to be there, but I was raw with grief from Logan's death. I spoke about Logan and his work with Tibetan refugees. I spoke of his passion for the environment and his concerns about global warming. I talked about the devastation of AIDS. I summoned his presence among us one last time.

Terry was there and so was Jamie Auchincloss, Jackie Kennedy's half-brother. After the service, Jamie drove us over to the Washington Mall where the National March for Lesbian and Gay Rights was in full swing. Hundreds of thousands of people participated in the march from all over the country. Despite my exhaustion, I felt exhilarated and empowered to be part of this moment in history: This was the first time that the AIDS Memorial Quilt was exhibited on the National Mall. At its inaugural exhibition, the Quilt's panels representing individuals who had died of AIDS covered an area the size of a small area of the mall. By the time of its last exhibition nearly nine years later, the panels covered the entire mall.

Logan's memorial service was held at St. Patrick's as he'd requested. Returning was a bittersweet experience. When I began working at St. Patrick's, I never imagined that in a few years I'd conduct funeral services there for friends fallen victim to an as yet unknown disease.

I had designed Logan's service a year earlier with him and his parents while he was in intensive care. The flower arrangements were exquisite. Music included a string quartet and an organ solo. Several of Logan's friends spoke, including straight friends from college and the Peace Corps whom he'd cut off when he began exploring gay life. Logan hadn't realized how much these people cared about him, regardless of his sexual orientation. They were hurt that he hadn't felt able to trust them. Their love for him was palpable.

It was a beautiful, poignant service. This was our last gift to Logan: We sent him off in style. He would have loved it. Afterwards, half a dozen of us gathered at an inexpensive Italian restaurant in the same Capitol Hill neighborhood where we'd lived next door to Logan several years before. We enjoyed a lasagna dinner served from a large casserole. As we were finishing up, someone noticed a used band-aid at the bottom of the pot. The juxtaposition of Logan's elegant memorial service and the used band-aid in the food at our dinner afterwards makes me laugh even today. Logan would never have let us dine in a cheap restaurant in the first place.

Logan was cremated in Virginia with a yellow rose on his chest. The rose was from a bush he had planted in his garden at the Sledz House. He'd given me custody of his ashes with clear instructions on what to do with them. He'd greatly admired the conservationist policies of President Theodore Roosevelt and was fond of a beautiful wooded island in the middle of the Potomac River named in his honor. Logan wanted some of his ashes scattered there, so a few weeks after his memorial service, four of us took them over. Two of that group would also die of AIDS within a few years.

Logan wanted the rest of his ashes scattered in the old cemetery at Christ Church in Cambridge, Massachusetts, where he'd attended graduate school at Harvard's John F. Kennedy School of Government. The summer following his death, I got together with one of Logan's old college friends, and we scattered the remaining ashes according to his wishes. While in Boston I met his former wife, Anne, and had a very poignant conversation about Logan.

CHAPTER TWENTY-THREE

RETREATS AND MINISTRIES

The night Logan died, while we were still gathered around him at the hospital, I got a call from the executive committee of ECRA telling me they'd raised enough money that they could now pay me a full-time salary. Under most circumstances, a pay raise is welcome news, but this meant that the epidemic was in full swing. I was in the belly of the beast. Logan would have been pleased that I was now getting a full-time salary.

Losing Logan haunted me for a long time. We had cherished each other. His death left an impressive absence, and I attempted to fill the vacuum with alcohol and pot. I never drank daily. I was what AA calls a "controlled drinker." I would go for three or four days without drinking, but I knew I'd make up for it on weekends or during my downtime. In earlier years, drinking and pot had served to boost my energy level, but now it wasn't having that same effect.

Spiritually, I was struggling to keep my head above water. The deaths were coming hard and fast, and visiting dying patients in hospitals was a routine part of my chaplaincy. We encountered ignorance and thinly veiled bigotry on a daily basis. It would have been easy to fall into despair.

Granted, there were moments of great satisfaction and happiness, because good things did happen in the midst of all the hard challenges. We achieved one of our greatest successes by teaming up with several other denominations to create an interfaith pastoral response to the crisis. Together, we designed a three-day retreat program for people living with AIDS.

Twenty-seven men joined us on our first retreat in November of 1987. They were all white and primarily young professionals.

Twenty-six of them were gay, and one claimed to be straight. In the years that followed, the demographics changed drastically. Increasingly, those attending our retreats were spread across the socio-economic spectrum and included women, drug addicts, Latinos, African Americans, and straights as well as gays.

We had trouble finding a retreat center that would allow us to use their facilities. Providentially, the Roman Catholic Diocese of West Virginia had a fine retreat center, Priest Field, about two hours from Washington, and they took us in. We were thrilled. It was a lovely place in the country and perfect for our needs.

We made the retreats inspirational and fun. We had good food and drink and enough activities to engage our clients without exhausting them. We offered inspirational speakers and small groups for emotional support. A popular feature was "talent night" when anyone who wanted to perform had an opportunity to put on a skit, sing a song, read a poem or otherwise entertain those present. We set aside an entire room for people to engage in creative activities like drawing, painting, sculpting, and writing. Talent night included a show-and-tell period during which people could talk about whatever they'd made in the "creativity" room. Many of our attendees had experienced shunning as a result of having AIDS. They were isolated because people were afraid to be near them. We were creating a space where they could be themselves, share their stories, and be touched.

On the last evening of each retreat, the staff decorated the dining hall and served a festive dinner. We presented each person with a gift. After dinner we conducted a healing service which included the laying on of hands and lots of hugging. We knew how important it was for people with AIDS to experience our caring through personal touch.

The template we created for that first retreat proved remarkably successful, so we continued to use it. Those weekends were magical. Each time the interfaith team and our clients returned from one of the retreats, we felt nurtured and restored. During the years of my AIDS ministry, I attended nearly 40 of these retreats. The power of those gatherings is with me still.

Other AIDS-based ministries were emerging to serve the

Washington, D.C. area. Damien Ministries was run by Lou Tesconi, a dynamic Roman Catholic who was HIV-positive. Food and Friends was a food service that fed many people too sick to prepare their own meals and was founded by a Presbyterian minister, Greta Reid. Both Lou and Greta were invaluable members of our retreat team.

The People with AIDS Coalition started up around that time, as well as Life Link, another AIDS support group. These groups sprang up like improbable flowers from rocky soil. Another such flower was The Carl Vogel Foundation, an organization that proved to be a great boon for my ministry with ECRA.

The eponymous Carl was a bright young man who'd grown up in Washington, attended the University of Virginia in the 1970s and, despite his slight build, had been a powerful crusader for gay rights. This meant taking a beating—literally—when he started a gay student group on the University of Virginia's Charlottesville campus. He was as gutsy as they come.

I met Carl in December of 1987 after he called me on the phone and said, "I have AIDS, I'm an Episcopalian, and I'd like to talk to you about doing my funeral." When I arrived to visit Carl at his father's house, it was obvious he had Kaposi's Sarcoma, a type of cancer suffered by many people with AIDS and character-ized by dark lesions on the skin. Carl's face was covered with purple splotches. It was the worst case I'd seen and covered his face like a ghoulish mask.

Carl recalled with irony the horror he'd felt several years earlier in San Francisco when he saw a man with AIDS receive communion from the common cup. "That was before I got sick myself, "he said. "And look at me now!" Carl was so honest about his personal history that it was hard not to like him.

He told me how funny he thought it would be if the bodies of young men who died of AIDS were dressed in drag before being shipped home to their families. Gallows humor certainly had its place during the epidemic. I had a chuckle and thought, "I could do that with my family."

Carl's family was loving and supportive. His father, Don Vogel, was a gruff, masculine guy who ran a construction com-pany with his other son, Mark. His sister, Paula Vogel, is an ac-claimed playwright who authored *The Baltimore Waltz* about a woman with a gay brother who suffers from a terminal illness. The play received positive critical reviews. I liked this family a lot. When Carl requested that a woman priest be involved with his funeral, I took Carole Crumley out to Maryland to meet him and his family. Carl liked Carole, so the visit went well—as well as a visit can go when you're planning the funeral of someone you like and admire. Carl died in January of 1988, and Carole and I conducted the funeral in the Bethlehem Chapel at the Washington National Cathedral.

I'd continued to run our burgeoning ministry out of my home office in Northern Virginia, which had its disadvantages. Not long after Carl's funeral, his father called me and said, "I'm starting a non-profit named after my son. We're going to call it the Carl Vogel Foundation. I've just rented some office space in downtown Washington, and I want you to have some of it for your office space. We won't charge you."

Don Vogel's gift to our ministry was another in the series of angelic visitations that sustained my personal equilibrium and made our ministry more accessible and effective. I moved my office from my house to downtown Washington, just a block from the George Washington University Hospital where I was constantly visiting people with AIDS. The Carl Vogel Foundation was devoted to supporting new treatments for AIDS, advising patients on diet and lifestyle issues, and advocating for medical research. I served on its board for several years.

In February of 1988, I was invited to a meeting of the heads of AIDS ministries from around the country. The Episcopal Church in San Francisco had taken the lead in promoting AIDS awareness, and now the Bishop of California wanted us to brainstorm ways to educate the wider church. The fifteen of us who attended the conference found the experience mutually encouraging and empowering. We came up with a slogan: Our Church Has AIDS. We knew it was provocative and weren't surprised when we got some kickback from it. But it made our point. We needed to take responsibility for the welfare of our parishioners during this epidemic. We met again in Washington in May to finalize our strategy for securing enactment of AIDS-friendly resolutions and legislation by the Episcopal Church's General Convention to be held in Detroit, Michigan later that year.

CHAPTER TWENTY-FOUR

ITALY

I turned 46 on March 25th, 1988. Terry and I invited George Eatman and a friend of his to dinner at our house. George had been in the group of four who'd asked me to do the funeral for their friend Darryl back in 1984. Darryl was the young man whose parents didn't even know he was gay until they learned he was dying of AIDS. Since then, George had become one of the angels supporting our ministry and was serving on the board of the Episcopal Caring Response to AIDS.

It was unseasonably warm that March evening, so we were able to move outdoors for my birthday dinner and celebration. The food and company were just right. And yet, I was unhappy. I wasn't at peace. On my 46th birthday, the darkness of the world I now inhabited threatened to overwhelm me. As though sensing how dispirited I felt, George suddenly announced, "I'm renting an apartment in Florence for a couple of months. Why don't you come to visit?"

I immediately burst out with, "We will!" I became obsessed with getting away to Italy. Terry was not so keen. His career with the United States Information Agency was in high gear, and he traveled a lot already. But I hadn't been to Italy since 1970, and I'd never been to Florence, so we compromised. Terry would come with me to Florence for our visit with George and then go on to Cairo for work; I would return to Washington on my own.

It all seemed like a good idea at the time. Only later did I appreciate the full significance of what was happening.

I think I was trying to save my relationship with Terry by doing something exciting together and by getting away from the epidemic for at least a little while. I was also trying to save myself. Life had become too much, and I grabbed on to the prospect of visiting Florence as a way out.

Although I'd not acknowledged the sickness in my soul even to myself, others were more attuned. Within two weeks before I left for Florence, three different women I knew approached me separately and wanted to know if I had AIDS. One woman, Debbie, told me she'd heard it on the radio. Although I doubted that was true—after all, Debbie had AIDS dementia—it hit a nerve. Another woman who inquired after my health was a genuinely concerned psychologist on the board of ECRA. The third was Jean Rogers, a budding priest and close ally. They sensed there was something wrong with me and reasoned it might be AIDS. These inquiries after my health felt like a warning and were deeply disconcerting.

We made it to Florence without incident and were soon entranced by the city's charms. One evening Terry, George and I were invited to dinner with several members of the American Episcopal Church in Florence. As we walked to the apartment of the member hosting our gathering, I began thinking about the evening ahead. I knew there'd be plenty of alcohol but suspected, as we strolled along the cobbled streets, that nobody else would be smoking marijuana. Not using the best judgement, I'd brought some pot on the plane with me. In those years, you could travel without being searched three times before so much as boarding an aircraft. I'd taken some to Paris in 1985, and this seemed no different.

I was determined to get a hit from my stash before arriving at the dinner party. I scooted on ahead, trying to find an alcove to duck into, but none was forthcoming. In desperation, I crouched down between two small Italian cars and lit up. I looked up and noticed I was right next to the Pitti Palace, a royal residence dating back to the middle ages. At that moment, a little voice in my head whispered with utter clarity, "This is pathetic." I knew then and there I had to do something about my addictions.

I summoned my courage and had a talk with Terry before we both left Italy. I let him know that when I got home I intended to cut way back on my drinking and smoking marijuana. I was true to my word. As I indulged less and less in drinking and smoking, my mind cleared, and my heart felt lighter. My depression began to lift. I became aware of the extent to which I'd blunted my emotions with drugs.

One awareness led to another. As I confronted my addictions,

I realized that Terry and I had been growing apart. When he got on the plane from Florence to Cairo, I noticed I was relieved we weren't going to be flying home together.

When Terry returned from his assignment in Egypt, we drove out to his parents' farm in Virginia, a place we'd always loved to visit. This time we were just going through the motions. When we returned home, we got into a big argument. This wasn't uncommon for us. Frequently, after we'd been partying all night, we'd get into a fight that would last the entire drive home. Alcohol made me verbally aggressive, and it made Terry sarcastic.

After we broke up, friends told me that they'd always felt uncomfortable when Terry and I went at it publicly. In the past, our cyclic arguments had seemed to be part of the glue that was holding us together. Now that I wasn't drinking so much, it was obvious we were arguing because we were unhappy. I went to the file cabinet and pulled out an agreement prepared for us by a lawyer back in 1977. It laid out how Terry and I would settle our affairs if we ever decided to split up. I said, "We need to read this." And it was as simple as that.

I didn't stop drinking completely until the end of 1988, but I was already feeling so much better that I knew quitting would be the right decision. I now had more energy, was more upbeat, and felt free. But my new-found enthusiasm was soon tempered by the news that Terry was seeing someone else. There was no thought of reconciliation, but the finality of our separation plunged me into grief for what we had lost.

The seeds of our discontent had been planted years before when I was doing hospital chaplaincy in Chicago and Terry was working as an interior designer. One evening, after an exhausting day of blood and gore and dying babies, I came home to find Terry all excited about his latest project. He'd been hired by a couple to design the interior of their house, and he'd done some beautiful sketches that were spread out on the table. The feelings it triggered were as involuntary as they were unfair. I was turned off by the superficiality of his work compared to my own. The contrast between the profound suffering I encountered on a daily basis at the hospital and the niceties of home décor heightened my perception of the differences between us. My self-absorption further intensified my sense of the disparity in the ways we'd chosen to lead our professional lives.

I never said anything to Terry about how I felt, but over time he picked up on my private self-righteousness. He would sometimes say, "I feel lonely in this relationship" or "I don't think we have enough in common." He'd always loved opera, while I didn't, and that bothered him. Alas, I was a kid who'd grown up in a coal mining town. I didn't attend my first opera until I was in college.

As idyllic as my childhood had been, it was isolating for a boy in the middle of the 20th century. Psychologically, I was born at the bottom of a coal mine shaft and spent the first eighteen years of my life climbing out of it. As soon as I got to ground level, I started to run. I ran to college and never looked back. But I did not grow up, as Terry had, as the child of educated and cosmopolitan parents.

Our lack of commonality was one of the elements that eventually broke us up. At the height of the AIDS epidemic, Terry rightly claimed I had become obsessed with the work I was doing. Our differences had been there from the beginning, but the divide became insurmountable during the plague years, and we grew apart.

That last summer as our relationship drew to its close, I got a call from Mike Crease, a friend of Logan's, who was still mourning him, as was I. Mike invited me to his small apartment for dinner that evening. After a good dinner, we talked late into the night, and I began nodding off. Mike offered me the guest room for a rest. After lying down, I saw hanging on the wall in front of me a lovely painting of a field of poppies. Mike was a talented artist, and several of his works were on display, but this one in particular caught my eye. Logan had been not only a friend but a mentor to Mike and had taken him to Europe several years before. The painting of the poppies was from their time together in France. The dancing poppies lifted my heart and caused me to think of the transition in my life with Terry in a new way.

It dawned on me that while Logan was dead, Mike was very much alive and continuing to create beautiful works of art inspired, in part, by his friendship and travels with Logan. Logan's legacy lived on. And even though my relationship with Terry had come to an end, I got to keep all of the good that had come from our years together. Why continue to be so upset at what had been lost when so much had been gained? I was alive, Terry was alive, and we had the rest of our lives before us. The mooring lines had been cut, and we could now sail forward in our own directions. I'd been set free, but not adrift.

CHAPTER TWENTY-FIVE

THE GENERAL CONVENTION

In 1987, a group of us had approached Charles Perry, the provost at the Washington National Cathedral, asking him to designate an area in one of the chapels for prayer for AIDS sufferers and their families, a request that he refused. Now, a year later, the ever-larger AIDS Quilt was going to be exhibited at the Washington Mall once again. A small group of us from my ministry took another approach and began to meet with Kwasi Thornell, an assistant to Provost Perry and a canon of the cathedral. We wanted to conduct an interfaith AIDS service to commemorate the Quilt exhibition, and we wanted the Gay Men's Chorus to perform a solo piece.

At our first meeting with Kwasi, a member of our group described how the proposed service would unfold. As soon as she mentioned a performance by the Gay Men's Chorus, Kwasi became visibly anxious. He expressed doubt that this would be permitted and said he'd have to talk with the provost. I listened to his vacillations with increasing anger. I didn't say anything, because I knew this was only the opening skirmish of a larger battle that would be fought at a later time. But I said to myself, "You'll stop this over my dead body." We decided to bypass the provost entirely and discuss the matter directly with the bishop, who outranked him. For the present, we had to focus on more immediate concerns.

In the summer of 1988, the Episcopal Church held its triennial General Convention in Detroit. This was the key event around which our national group of AIDS ministries had been strategizing for months. The group had two goals: the first was to represent ourselves with a booth, like any other conventioneer; the second, to lobby for legislation within the church to recognize the AIDS epidemic and to pursue gay rights.

The General Convention, the primary governing body of the Episcopal Church, is a bicameral legislature of about a thousand members consisting of a House of Deputies made up of laypeople, deacons and priests elected from each diocese and a House of Bishops comprised of bishops from those dioceses. Its structure and operation are similar to those of the U.S. Congress with its House of Representatives and Senate. Both houses of the convention have to pass legislation in identical form for it to be enacted as church law.

Coincidentally, the AIDS Memorial Quilt was in Detroit at the same time as the General Convention. It was put on display in one of the big halls at the convention site. Each of the Quilt's individual panels was three feet wide and six feet long and represented a person who had died of AIDS. The panels were sewn together to make up larger squares that comprised the Quilt. The Quilt became much, much larger over time, but in 1988 it merely filled a large convention hall. At the exhibit's opening, the panels had been folded and placed within their own squares inside the Quilt. As each name of an individual who'd died of AIDS was read aloud volunteers reverently unfolded each of the large squares containing the panels.

It was a solemn and powerfully symbolic unfolding. The day before the Quilt was exhibited, another young priest and I ran around Detroit handing out press releases to the news outlets hoping to interest them in covering the event. We were successful beyond our dreams. The exhibition was swarmed by media – newspapers, radio, and television. You name it, they were there.

The chief pastor and spokesperson for the Episcopal Church in the United States is its Presiding Bishop. The "P.B." is responsible for developing ecclesiastical policy and administering of the church on the national level. In 1988, our Presiding Bishop was Edmund Browning. Ed was a strong pastor who worked hard to realize the vision of a more caring and inclusive church. He was soft-spoken, but he didn't pull his punches. At his installation as presiding bishop in Washington National Cathedral a year earlier, I heard him proclaim that, "In this church, there shall be no outcasts." You could have heard a pin drop. A woman behind me whispered to her friend, "He's talking about homosexuals." Indeed, he was.

The morning of the ceremonial unfolding of the Quilt, Bishop Browning made a statement before the TV cameras that the church's response to AIDS was one of compassion. He then presided over a healing service attended by 700 people where I was one of the healers. As I laid hands on the heads of those before me and prayed for their healing, I was reminded again of my Pentecostal roots. The irony didn't escape me. After years of moving far beyond the Holy Roller practices of my youth, here I was participating in one of their most time-honored traditions - under the auspices of the Presiding Bishop of the Episcopal Church, no less. My ancestors had been on to something worthy and true all along.

The Presiding Bishop blessed the panels that were to be added to the Quilt, then he led a solemn procession to the large hall where the Quilt was displayed. We processed around the edge of the Quilt, led by a cross and candles with ten priests following the bishop. Behind us were people carrying the panels that would be added to the Quilt. I cried the whole way. There was a panel in the Quilt for my friend Logan, whose death continued to weigh heavily on my mind and heart. As we processed, I was wearing the Cartier watch he'd given me. I felt mystically transported for the entire service. I felt God's presence as clearly as if I'd been with Jesus at the moment of his transfiguration.

A reporter for a local television station grabbed me and started an interview right there in front of a camera. I can't remember a word of my mumbled response. I'm sure all they saw in that moment was a grieving priest doing an imitation of Tammy Faye Baker in tears. If I'd worn mascara, it would have trailed down my cheeks.

By the time we returned to our hotel, my sadness had been replaced by joy as I reflected on the day's events. Another priest, Skip Schueddig, and I had been working our butts off for days, and we were ready for a break. We gave ourselves some time off and decided to take it easy for a few hours. I went up to Skip's room to change before heading down to the pool, and we both realized we weren't yet done processing the day's events. We talked about our experiences for half an hour or so, and I began to feel my eyelids drooping. I hadn't slept much the night before, and the summer heat was sapping my consciousness.

Skip went on down for a swim, and I fell asleep. Before dozing off, I removed Logan's gold Cartier watch that I'd been wearing constantly for the past two years. I lay across the bed and set the watch on the carpet before falling fast asleep. After at least an hour of deep sleep, I woke up feeling groggy and disorientated and headed off to the pool to find Skip. We swam, and as I was drying off I realized I'd forgotten the watch. We went back up to the room, but it was gone. I reported the theft, but the watch was never recovered. When I reported my lost watch to Bob, one of my more mystical friends, he responded that some people believe loved ones from the other side come and take their gifts back.

I spent nine days in Detroit, and they were among the most exhilarating days of my life. Despite the lost watch, I returned to Washington inspired and strengthened for the challenges that lay yet ahead. Our group of AIDS ministry leaders, formed only months before in San Francisco, had never worked a General Convention before this one. We held strategy meetings, issued press releases, attended hearings and testified on behalf of proposed legislation. This General Convention was our first opportunity to pursue our goals with the national church, and we were delighted with our successes. Based partly on our recommendations, the Convention appointed an official Joint Commission on AIDS for the church. It also established the National Episcopal AIDS Coalition to continue lobbying for effective AIDS ministries at all levels of the church.

We'd done good work, and I forged friendships with other AIDS warriors that have lasted to this day.

CHAPTER TWENTY-SIX

Ron Bushnell

Terry and I had agreed not to sell our house until after the first of the year. We were both constantly on the move, and our careers had us working all hours. He was traveling, and I was building my AIDS ministry. We needed time to sell the house, and we needed a place to live while we sorted out how we would separate.

I'd been driving a small Toyota Tercel for several years—an appropriate car for a priest, although I drove it like a bat out of hell. It was getting a little worn, so I decided it was time for a new car. Call it a mid-life crisis if you like, but after a lot of research, I went out and bought a more luxurious Toyota Supra. I loved that car. It drove like a dream. I found a used one only two years old and bought it off a well-to-do college kid for $20,000. That was a small fortune then, but my research reliably informed me that Supras were underpriced and a great value. I drove that car until it died under me many years later in Miami.

I had a new car, and I was about to have a new partner. I first encountered Ron Bushnell on the very same weekend I bought that Toyota Supra, and thereby hangs a tale.

In the fall of 1987, I was asked by a lovely young man in his thirties, Robert Thompson, to help him plan his funeral. Robert was gay and had AIDS. He'd grown up in a large southern family but had been living in New York until his diagnosis. He'd returned to his Virginia roots to die.

I drove out to Northern Virginia to meet with Robert and was captivated immediately. He was charming, had a great sense of humor, and was an altogether delightful human being. I visited him at home over the next several months and then at the hospital as his condition deteriorated. The last time I saw him in the hospital, he was in bed smoking. How he managed that, I don't know, but he was. He had Kaposi's Sarcoma lesions on his face and didn't have much energy, but he was sitting up looking in a mirror. Contemplating his reflection, he remarked, "You know, you just can't improve on perfection." How can you not love someone with that kind of humor and courage?

Robert had grown up in Truro Episcopal Church, an historic mid-18th century parish in Fairfax, Virginia, and he wanted to have his funeral in its chapel. I knew immediately that it wouldn't be easy. Truro had become a bastion of conservatism in the Episcopal Church and was actively involved in the pro-life movement. The parish was anti-gay and even started a conversion therapy program to convert homosexuals to a heterosexual orientation. Truro was part of a new wave of charismatic Episcopal churches and was militant in its activism. Some charismatic churches were liberal or progressive, but not the majority and certainly not this one.

I encountered this phenomenon repeatedly in my ministry. Gay men from conservative churches sought to find solace at the end of their lives, only to be discriminated against for their sexual orientation or because of the fear and superstition surrounding AIDS. I didn't want to dash Robert's hopes entirely, but I knew the situation was problematic, and we had to be realistic. I explained the direction the church had taken since Robert's childhood and then gave him some options. "We could go and plead with the rector to have mercy on us," I suggested, "or we could just let it be for now, and when the time comes, I'll try to finesse it." He chose the latter.

When Robert died in August of 1988 I called the Truro parish and explained the situation to the secretary. She told me she would have to talk to the rector and get back to me. Coincidentally, I was about to leave for the Washington National Cathedral where I was part of a planning committee for an upcoming AIDS healing service, so I gave her the cathedral's phone number to call me back on. Apparently, the rector recognized the number. When the secretary called me back, she said, "The rector says yes, you can have the funeral here on Saturday." I hung up and let out a big sigh of relief.

On Saturday morning, I arrived early at the chapel in my

newly purchased Toyota Supra and a clerical collar. I hadn't actually seen the chapel and wanted to check it out before the service. I was greeted by a young, rosy-cheeked, straight priest with a strong handshake and immediately started praying that he'd want nothing to do with the service. He showed me through the chapel and then he said, "Now, what exactly do you do at the National Cathedral?"

I just wanted to get done what needed to be done, so I shamelessly dropped some names before adding, "I'm not on the actual staff at the cathedral. I'm Chaplain of the Episcopal Caring Response to AIDS, the AIDS ministry for the diocese." Mercifully, he went away, and I considered it one of my great pastoral victories. Robert would have his funeral in the chapel that he loved.

The night before, at the funeral home, Robert's casket had been surrounded by floral arrangements. There must have been seventy-five of them, representing a prodigious outpouring of love. Too often, AIDS funerals reflected a great deal of rejection and shame as families put up defensive walls against an unwelcome reality. This was not the case at Robert's funeral. The Truro Chapel was filled with his family and friends and their love for him.

I sat to one side in my vestments as various people came up to speak about Robert. That's when I saw Ron Bushnell for the first time. Up from the congregation came this handsome, 28-year-old man in a dark blue pinstriped suit with fashionable slice cuts in his hair. He stood beside Robert's casket and spoke with eloquence and grace from his heart. He told us that he was a member of Robert's HIV support group, and that they'd become good friends. At the end of his remarks, he said, "I will be joining you soon, Robert." I thought, "No, this can't be."

I was enchanted. I just wanted to go over and hold him. Though I noticed Ron that day, we wouldn't actually meet for another month.

In September, we held another AIDS retreat at Priest Field in West Virginia, and Ron attended. Everybody dressed down at the retreats, so I wasn't wearing my clerical collar. Ron wasn't wearing a coat and tie but only shorts and a T-shirt and was being very playful. I didn't recognize him, and he didn't recognize me.

At one point during the retreat, I came across Ron practicing Reiki meditation techniques with a small group of people. Ron was an experienced meditator and had a gift for leading guided meditation exercises. His sister once told me that he seemed surrounded by radiant light throughout his childhood, always smiling and irrepressibly playful. He never lost those qualities. I was drawn by his energy into his meditation circle, and then I was drawn to him. He felt vaguely familiar to me, but I couldn't place how I might have come across him before.

On the second day of our retreat, Ron and I took a walk together along the creek that ran through the property. It was a beautiful afternoon, and we soon found ourselves intimately engaged in conversation. As we talked, Ron began to pick up trash and old soda cans, passing them on to me when his own hands were full. I hardly noticed. By the time we finished our walk, we both had armfuls of trash. To this day I pick up trash because of Ron Bushnell.

Our conversation continued unabated when we got back to the retreat center, picked up again after dinner, and extended late into the night before we tumbled into bed and into each other's arms.

By the time the retreat ended, everybody knew we were heavily into each other. This created a bit of a crisis for me because at least two of the interfaith staff members strongly disapproved. In their view, it was wrong for me, a priest in a position of authority, to be "taking advantage of a 28-year-old victim of AIDS." I was 46, so there was an age difference, but as far as I was concerned, their argument stemmed from the fact that the church has never been comfortable with sex, even though it's had hundreds of years in which to think it through. Their disapproval felt like Puritanism run amok. In any event, Ron was an adult, our relationship was consensual, and it lasted for the rest of Ron's life.

Later that week after returning from the retreat, Ron invited me over for a romantic dinner at his house. In the course of our conversation that night, he mentioned that a close friend, Robert Thompson, had just died and that he had spoken at his funeral.

"Good grief," I exclaimed. "You spoke at his funeral? But I was the priest that officiated at his funeral!"

Ron couldn't believe I was the priest who'd officiated at the service, insisting "That priest was straight, and he was wearing a yellow dress."

"Well," I said, "I'm not straight, and that wasn't a yellow dress!" Then we both laughed at our mutual mistake.

The "yellow dress" was actually a cope made of white silk brocade that had belonged to my college chaplain, Fred Norman, and was given to me by his widow after he died. Apparently, the white had turned a bit yellow with age. Whenever Ron recounted that story, the "yellow dress" featured prominently.

I fell madly in love with Ron and his larger-than-life personality, and he with me. He was 5-foot 10-inches tall, handsome with an engaging smile, and oozed boyish charm. He had been diagnosed with full-blown AIDS the year before and nearly died from pneumocystis pneumonia. Doctors diagnosed AIDS as "full-blown" when a person infected by the HIV virus had a T-cell count lower than 200. The normal count is 500 to 1,500. T-cells are important to the immune system, so when they are depleted, the body becomes vulnerable to opportunistic infections such as Ron's pneumonia. These infections are the cause of death for most AIDS patients.

By the time I met Ron, he'd fought off the pneumonia and was the picture of health. He had initially lost a lot of weight but not his sense of humor. By taking good care of himself, he had worked himself back to a strapping 180 pounds.

After his AIDS diagnosis, Ron feared he'd never have the chance to experience a loving, committed relationship. Fate decreed otherwise. From our first night together until the day he died, we loved each other with passionate intensity. After dating for several months, we began living together in April of 1989.

Ron worked hard to maintain his health after his diagnosis. That hadn't always been the case. He'd been quite the party boy working as a model and a go-go dancer before getting sober at the age of 24. By the time I met him, he ate well, exercised, meditated, and prayed. He'd been a member of Alcoholics Anonymous for four years, and the twelve steps of the program helped discipline his life. Although he was on disability and unable to work at a regular job, he managed to go back to school and complete his BA degree in liberal arts.

Notwithstanding Ron's good example, I hadn't taken the plunge myself. I was doing what people in AA call "white knuckling," trying to get sober by myself. I hadn't yet surrendered my will and my life to a "higher power," one of the twelve steps of AA.

Ron was one of several people who appeared in my life after declaring my intention to sober up. A therapist friend of mine had invited me to attend his weekly twelve steps of AA meeting at the Friend's Meeting House. It was for anyone who wanted to learn about the twelve steps. There also were three members of AA who began attending the Thursday healing service at the cathedral. We started having breakfast after the service where I would ask lots of questions about AA. It was as if I had unconsciously invited them into my life to help me in my transition.

In the fall of 1988, we attended a big fundraising dinner for the Human Rights Campaign, a national lobbying group for gay rights. Anyone who was anyone in the gay community was there, and I quickly learned that Ron was my perfect political partner. He knew half the people, and I knew the other half, which became increasingly clear as we worked our way around the room. Of course, he was telling everybody how much he was in love with me.

That October, we traveled up to New York City to attend a workshop conducted by Louise Hay, a well-known motivational speaker who helped people think more constructively about their lives and develop positive approaches to recovering from illness and returning to health. Ron was a huge fan. We'd heard about her weekly support groups called "Hay Rides" at St. Thomas Episcopal Church in Hollywood, California. Hundreds of gay men attended these events, and when she scheduled a weekend workshop in Manhattan, we just had to be there.

We participated in her workshop and had a great time doing so. We stayed with my friend Mitch Dafner who would later die of AIDS but was healthy at the time. We walked around the city, found some great restaurants, and even got tickets to the musical hit *Into the Woods*, which was playing on Broadway. Ron and I were utterly in love. In the midst of the hell that was AIDS, we found ourselves briefly in heaven. It was a lovely weekend in every way, a gift that helped carry us through some hard times ahead.

Although Louise caught a lot of criticism from some circles for giving what they considered to be "false hope" to people with AIDS, I thought she was great. I saw gay men with AIDS change their outlook dramatically for the better after attending her seminars.

In 1988, AIDS was a death sentence. Outsiders might have viewed the relationship Ron and I shared in tragic terms, but only if they didn't know Ron. Sally Fischer, who became well known for facilitating "AIDS Mastery" workshops across the country, told me when Ron died, "Ron was the most alive person I've ever met." Although he could be serious when the occasion called for it, he was usually in a playful mood, laughing and hugging and joking, sometimes using bawdy humor. Because he refused to wallow in self-pity for even a moment, others were challenged to rise above the grimness of their lives right along with him. He was an incredible inspiration until the end of his life. He remains so for me even now.

The subject of our sex life came up often in conversation with friends. People would ask me point blank, "Aren't you afraid you'll catch it?" It became a common refrain. We all had friends who'd stopped having sex because of their fear. Giving up sex entirely seemed safer and easier than living in constant fear of catching the deadly disease.

In the early years, we didn't know exactly how the AIDS virus was transmitted. People feared it could be contracted by kissing, touching or even by being in the same room as someone suffering with the disease. Slowly, as research progressed, the medical profession reached a consensus that AIDS was most often spread through unprotected anal sex. The key to protection against infection was avoiding the exchange of body fluids by practicing "safer" sex. Condom use became the new norm.

Although the findings of medical science on AIDS weren't yet definitive, the evidence that infection could be avoided by practicing safer sex was encouraging. It helped me conquer my own fears, and perhaps what I lacked in fear I made up for in naiveté. In any case, Ron and I had great sex. Sometimes it takes courage to love.

It takes courage to skydive, too, and that had been at the top of Ron's bucket list. That fall he not only jumped from an airplane, but jumped into my arms. That first year we were together, he was scheduled to speak at an AA meeting, and I went with him as a guest. He was entertaining and funny as he talked about AA's concept of surrender and tied it in with his skydiving experience. Surrender is a key element of the twelve step program. He described how, when it came his turn to leap out of the plane into the unknown, he refused to jump. "Then," he said, "a butch woman shoved me out the door, and I screamed all the way to the ground." Ron was so charismatic when he spoke that he had the 150 people at the meeting in the palm of his hand. It was the first time I saw him speak at an AA meeting, and it was obvious he engaged people's hearts along with their minds.

CHAPTER TWENTY-SEVEN

THE SERVICE AND
THE QUILT

In October of 1988, the Washington Mall welcomed the long-awaited return of the AIDS Memorial Quilt. Our AIDS ministry had made great progress in planning an accompanying interfaith healing service at the National Cathedral, but we still didn't know whether Bishop Walker would allow the Gay Men's Chorus to sing a solo anthem. We'd been left to hold our collective breath and wait.

Finally, in an act that circumvented Provost Charles Perry, the bishop met directly with several members of the chorus. Still, he didn't make up his mind. There was a lot of anxiety and ill will about the bishop's vacillation on this matter, and the chorus leadership threatened to pull out of the service entirely. They were a top-notch choral group and didn't appreciate being judged or jerked around. I begged them to be patient. I knew they'd be able to participate in the service as a group but wasn't yet sure if they'd be able to sing a solo anthem.

The bishop's reluctance to overrule his provost stirred up emotions I thought I'd long since laid to rest. About ten days before the planned interfaith service to commemorate the quilt, I was overwhelmed by feelings of shame while driving to our Thursday morning healing service. I fell right back where I'd started in the bad old days before hard-earned self-acceptance through years of therapy made it possible to live with integrity and pride. I could hear judgmental voices in my mind berating me with, "Who do you think you are? Do you know what you're asking for? You're asking too much. You're nothing."

When I got to the cathedral, I walked up the dark, hidden

staircase that leads to the rear of the sacristy, the room where we were to vest. With every step, my feelings of shame turned to rage. I wanted to murder Charles Perry, the provost who was making life so difficult for those of us trying to make the church a more welcoming place for people with AIDS. I'd never before faced celebrating the Holy Communion in a state of outraged fury. Yet here I was, preparing to say mass with my co-celebrant Carole Crumley and a laywoman who was there to assist us. I couldn't even share my feelings with them. I was too angry and embarrassed to speak.

The National Cathedral is neo-Gothic in design and modeled on the English Gothic style of the late middle ages. It has ten different chapels, and our healing services were held in Bethlehem Chapel, the first of them to be built. As we made our way down the stairway leading to the chapel, I struggled within to find a state of grace. All I found was fury.

As I began the service with the opening words of the liturgy, a voice within spoke the words I needed to hear: "Pray for him." So, I did. I prayed for Charles Perry. In our Prayers of the People, there's an opportunity for members of the clergy and congregation to call out the names of those for whom prayers are requested. As soon as I spoke aloud his name, "Charles," my prayer for grace was answered. My anger drained away. This surprised me.

My serenity restored, I was able to proceed with the communion service in good conscience. Facing the altar, I began the prayer of consecration over the elements of bread and wine. As I had done so many times before, I repeated the words spoken by Jesus at the Last Supper, "This is my body, this is my blood, given for you." But this time I fully registered that I, Jerry Anderson, was included in the gift. Christ's body and blood were given not just for others, but for me. I'd long known this intellectually, of course, but this realization on a deeper emotional level pierced my defenses and opened my heart. I had an overwhelming sense of God's presence surrounding us in the chapel. I began to weep. I was grateful that my back was to the congregation because I didn't want them to see my tears.

In the sacristy after the service, I described my experience to Carole Crumley and Peggy, the laywoman who had assisted us. They recounted that they had similarly felt God's presence during the service. Remarkably, Carol even stated that she was floating above the chapel looking down on us. It was a mystical encounter with the Holy that the three of us shared that day, and one I've treasured in memory ever since.

Since Ron had come into my life, my heart was more open than ever before. The love we shared lifted me to a higher spiritual plane. My transformation from a state of rage to forgiveness toward Charles Perry is one of the most profound experiences of God's grace I've ever had.

After months of planning, we were fully prepared for our interfaith healing service to accompany the quilt's exhibition on the National Mall. The service was scheduled for a Sunday afternoon in early October. In the end, the bishop did not allow the chorus to sing a solo anthem, but they were allowed to process as a group in their tuxedos and to sing along with everyone else. To my great relief, the chorus decided against boycotting the service and agreed to participate in the event.

Thousands of people showed up to see the quilt on the Mall, and 4,000 of them turned up at the cathedral for our service. The congregation overwhelmed the interior space and spilled outside through the doors. It seemed that every sort and condition of humanity was represented by those in attendance. There were people with AIDS and those who loved them. There were people who were marginalized and unloved and others who came from money and power. Believers from multiple nationalities, races, and faiths joined non-believers in the pews. The mixed demographic signaled that our message was being heard in many different places. I truly felt this was a foretaste of heaven.

TV cameras rolled, and I ran around like a chicken with its head cut off trying to pull everything together while giving interviews on the fly. Chip Aldridge, Logan's former AIDS buddy with whom I'd remained close, helped bring me down to earth. He appeared at my side in the midst of the pre-service hubbub and let me know he'd brought along some of Logan's ashes. I was surprised to learn we hadn't scattered them all and delighted to have Logan symbolically present on this momentous occasion.

The philanthropist Bob Alfandre had commissioned an artist to make an AIDS panel for his deceased partner, Carroll Sledz, and Ron carried it as a banner during the procession. Ron was seated in the front row of the nave, and I was sitting in the choir across from him. Throughout the service, he kept blowing kisses at me. At some point later in the service, he kissed me on the cheek. It was difficult to maintain my solemn demeanor under the circumstances.

The people who'd accused me of taking advantage of Ron two months earlier had no idea how much he was the one actually steering our relationship. His demonstrative love for me at this ground-breaking event was nothing short of exhilarating. I'd lived in a dark place for a long time, and our love for each other marked the beginning of a welcome shift in the quality of my life.

The highlight of our service was yet to come. We'd arranged five or six healing stations around the nave of the cathedral with several ministers at each station. When the time came for the healing part of the service, hundreds of members of the congregation came forward to receive the laying on of hands. They would explain why they wanted healing, and the ministers would lay hands on them and pray for them to be restored to health.

This part of the service went on for a long time, and I could only marvel at how much it resembled an old-fashioned revival meeting from my childhood. My Grandmother Anderson—a fervent Pentecostal until the day she died—would have been pleased with her grandson.

CHAPTER TWENTY-EIGHT

ALCOHOLICS ANONYMOUS

Many people mistakenly believe that an alcoholic is someone who wakes up each morning and can't stop drinking until he passes out. That's true of some alcoholics, but many manage to function at a fairly high level. I fell into the latter category. I was what's known in AA as a "controlled drinker." I thought I had my drinking under control, so I didn't consider it a problem. It's common for alcoholics to avoid dealing with the fact that they're abusing alcohol if they're able to get up each morning and go to work without getting fired.

Over the years, friends had occasionally tried to talk to me about my drinking, but I'd ignored them. At my first parish, I formed a close friendship with a couple, Ray and Jean, who often invited me over for dinner and conversation. Ray and I became fast friends and drinking buddies. We preferred hard liquor. One day, Ray's worried 14-year-old son pointed out to his father that he drank so much that it was obvious even to him that he had a problem. Motivated by his son's concern, Ray eventually got into rehab and became sober. I was shocked at the news, but it never occurred to me that I, too, was drinking to excess.

Years later Jean visited Washington on business, and we got together for dinner. In the course of the evening she gingerly asked me about my own drinking. My response was automatic. I assured her I had it under control. Others had raised concerns along the way, but I dismissed them all.

My family and the Pentecostal church had always condemned alcohol, so drinking was high on the list of forbidden behaviors to indulge in once I got away to college. When I began drinking my first week away from home, I felt an immediate sense of liberation from the repressive prohibitions of my childhood. My Pentecostal church was uncompromisingly strict, and this first step to breaking out of its bonds gave me a rush—a dangerous association when it comes to alcohol. When I did get sober, years later, drinking no longer gave me a sense of freedom. It had enslaved me.

My introduction to AA came while I was serving at St. Patrick's Church. A parish friend invited me to join him at a meeting one night, and I accepted the opportunity to see what it was like. That particular evening, the two speakers talked about their struggles with alcohol and then shared their sources of strength and hope in overcoming their addiction. The room was filled with smoke, so it felt like being in a bar. There was also lots of laughter, which lightened my spirit. When we left the meeting, I said to my friend, "I feel a lot better, and when I'm feeling depressed again I'll attend another meeting." I didn't go back for a long time, but the writing was on the wall.

That New Year's Eve marked a radical departure from the past. For years, Terry and I had celebrated the occasion by hosting a black-tie dinner at our house. Our annual tradition was a highlight of the year and for me included lots of booze and grass. That year Terry and I would celebrate the holiday apart, in different styles and in different places. I was relieved.

Every New Year's Eve, one of our AIDS ministry benefactors, Melody Gilsey, hosted a big gala event to raise funds for different charities. These galas were held at the Four Seasons Hotel, and they were all beautifully done. That first year without Terry, I invited a good friend, Ken Lauden, to go with me. Ken had been part of Logan's support team and was one of the most healthy, athletic people I'd ever known. We had a terrific time at the gala. It was a great dinner with congenial company and lovely music. We had no idea that Ken himself would die of AIDS within four years.

Melody always reserved a block of rooms for her gala at the Four Seasons, and she'd offered one to me. I stayed the night in luxurious surroundings, feeling as good the next morning as I had when I went to bed. My head was as clear as a bell. It had been decades—probably since my Pentecostal Bible college days— since I'd woken up sober on New Year's Day. I was alert and vital, free of depression and happy to be alive. I'd entered a whole new reality. What a great way to start the year!

It didn't last. A few days later as I was sitting in my office on a gray Washington morning, Terry called to tell me that he and his new boyfriend Chuck were going to Atlanta to visit Jodie and Pete Gonzales. Terry and Jodie had been college classmates, and we'd all gotten to know each other well over the years. I'd baptized their two girls at the National Cathedral, so we were good friends. When I learned Terry would be visiting them with someone else, I was hit by a wave of depression. I felt that something precious was being stolen from me. I knew that wasn't rational, but depression doesn't rely on logic. I felt that I was the one who should be going.

Within moments the thought came to me, "I wonder who's having a party tonight? Where can I go to get drunk?"
In the clutches of a panic attack, I called Ron gripping the phone with white knuckles. "Are you going to an AA meeting tonight?" I asked. "Can I join you?"

I began crying as soon as I hung up the phone. I don't think I stopped for two weeks, it was so cathartic.

On a cold snowy night I met Ron at a Presbyterian church in Georgetown and attended my first AA meeting as a seeker, not an observer. It was a small meeting of perhaps 15 people. It was a closed meeting, which meant that anyone who wasn't already an AA member shouldn't attend. But there I was. We were going around the table, and when my turn came I said something like, "I don't know if I'm an alcoholic or not, but I do know I'm addicted to marijuana."
Ron's sponsor was there. He was a crusty old by-the-book sort of guy, and he was straight. Later, in the kitchen, he let Ron have it for bringing me to a closed meeting. Meanwhile, another man handed me his business card and said, "You know, marijuana is what got me into these meetings. If you want to talk, call me." So, I did, and he became my first sponsor.

Ron informed me later that night that AA strongly encourages newcomers to attend ninety meetings in the first ninety days of recovery. It was January 6th, which meant I'd be attending daily meetings into April.

I didn't think I could do it, but I did. Ron took me to a meeting the next day at a Methodist church, and that became my home group in Washington. I returned there on a recent visit to Washington to lead a meeting, and there were people who remembered Ron and me almost thirty years later. I wasn't surprised. That AA group was the lifeblood of my recovery, and Ron and I attended many meetings there together.

I was soon amazed by how much fun you could have without alcohol. As I progressed in my sobriety, I became newly aware of the world around me. I realized that I'd been living in an alternative universe for many years. The real world entranced me. I first noticed this one evening while driving through Rock Creek Park along a road much loved by Franklin D. Roosevelt. Suddenly the natural world felt imbued with a heretofore unseen beauty and charm. It was all so ordinary and yet extraordinarily vivid in my perception.

Although my father never joined AA, he had been a drinker in the years before he joined the Pentecostal church. I'd heard stories, but they were few and far between. I learned more after both my parents had died. One of my mother's younger sisters later told me that she'd been afraid of my father when he drank. She remembered his sometimes passing out on the front porch during the years of Prohibition when my grandfather had a moonshine still at his farmhouse.

As a sober member of Alcoholics Anonymous by the time I heard this story, I felt bonded with a part of my father's past that I'd never known in life. Years later, I thought of him while sitting on a beach in California watching the sun go down. I felt relaxed and contemplative. I sensed my father's presence in the quiet of dusk and felt a gentle communion with his spirit. Then came his words, "I forgive you for your drinking." I began sobbing with love and relief, then left to attend an AA meeting where I shared my experience.

CHAPTER TWENTY-NINE

A NEW ERA

President George H.W. Bush was inaugurated on January 20th, 1989. It was a cold, gray day. The gay and lesbian community had been frustrated and angered by the Reagan administration's failure to acknowledge the AIDS crisis and was hoping for a change. On election day of the previous year, Ron's friend Bob Gray had called to tell him he'd been invited to the White House to watch the election returns with the Reagans. Bob was gay and closeted and heading off to socialize with a president who refused to acknowledge the AIDS epidemic sweeping the country. Ron kept yelling into the phone, "Bob, just say the word, AIDS! Just say the word AIDS tonight at the White House!"

On Inauguration Day, Ron and I found ourselves in a well-situated Washington office across from the Treasury Building, right above the parade route. We stood and waved from the window as the incoming president went by in his limousine. One of the fun things about being in Washington is that you get to participate directly in these national celebrations that everybody else watches on television. You can be right in the middle of the action.

A week later, I got a call in my office from Julie Cooke who was working for the new First Lady, Barbara Bush. Julie was an Episcopalian and knew about our ministry. I was astonished and delighted by her news: "The First Lady has identified AIDS as one of the top issues she wants to be involved with. Can you help us?"

After eight long years of inaction by the Reagan administration, a new day had dawned. My group immediately put together a small committee to develop ideas, and on February 2nd we met with Barbara Bush's staff in the east wing of the White House to strategize ways in which the First Lady could be involved. At a second meeting soon after that, we politely suggested that Mrs. Bush consider visiting Grandma's House, a residence established by two women activists for children with AIDS.

By this time, after two years of hard work, Melody Gilsey had brought together a number of her friends and begun planning a major AIDS charity fundraising gala for the spring of 1989. We asked Mrs. Bush if she'd be willing to lend her name to the event by acting as honorary chair of the committee for the gala. Much to our delight, she agreed to do so. Having her name associated with the gala ensured good publicity for the event and a great turnout.

There were a couple of people on the board of the Episcopal Caring Response to AIDS who thought we should have nothing to do with the Bushes and that the First Lady's contributions were mere political window dressing. Fortunately, their shortsighted view was overruled. We weren't about to forfeit the support of the First Lady of the United Sates, so I moved ahead with our plans for the gala.

In early February, I secured permission from the Washington, D.C. Quaker community to use their Meeting House to hold memorial services for people who had died of AIDS. The Friends Meeting House was a lovely stone building in the Dupont Circle neighborhood, then a residential area for many of the city's gay population. I was to hold a number of memorial services and even a couple of weddings for gay partners there; it became a sacred space for me. I was grateful to the Quakers for their generosity and support.

Another of the blessings that emerged from the epidemic was that we began working across denominational lines to a much greater extent than ever before. ECRA had established a close relationship with Damien Ministries, the Roman Catholic group founded by Lou Tesconi and named after Father Damien, a priest who had lived and worked with lepers on Molokai Island in Hawaii. Through my connection with Lou, I was invited to concelebrate mass at Holy Trinity Catholic Church in Georgetown. The Roman Catholic Church does not officially recognize the validity of the Anglican priesthood or sacraments, so this was a special event. It was a beautiful service. As we priests—Roman Catholic and Episcopal—stood together for the consecration of the bread and wine, I felt as though we were making history. Going forward, I concelebrated mass a number of times with Roman Catholic priests, often at our retreats. Of course, there were many Catholic clergy who wouldn't concelebrate the mass with Episcopal priests, but generally speaking, the AIDS epidemic was breaking down barriers.

Early in the new year, Ron and I took a vacation to Florida, first to Miami and then to Key West. We spent a couple of nights with friends, Bob Gray and Bill Austin, then rented a car and drove over to Miami Beach. It was fun to be there while the old art deco hotels were being restored and before the area was horrendously over-developed as it is now. We drove down to the end of Ocean Drive and came upon the Betsy Ross Hotel. It was under renovation and had a big sign out front advertising rooms at $29.95 per night. As soon as Ron saw it, he said, "That's where we're staying!" We didn't have a lot of money, so it was just what we needed. We got a room on the second floor with decently sized windows, but we had to buy some Windex and paper towels to fully appreciate the view of the ocean.

We went to an AA speaker's meeting that night where a crusty old woman told her story. She was a recovering alcoholic with a husky, gravelly voice, and she was funny and poignant. She shared one of her deepest regrets, that her mother had died before she could see her daughter get sober and turn her life around. "If you have loved ones and you haven't told them you love them recently," she concluded, "tell them you love them now, before it's too late."

"Oh my God," I thought. "My mother's birthday is next week, and I haven't told my parents I'm sober!"

I'd done some drinking and smoking away from my mom and dad when I returned for visits. But mothers have their ways of knowing, and mine was no exception. From time to time, she'd bring up my drinking, and we'd get into an argument. The last time, when she'd raised the subject on the telephone, I'd hung up on her. But now, this delightful old lady's talk at an AA meeting spurred me to action. I went out and bought my mother a birthday card and included a letter to both my parents. I told them that I was in AA, that I was sober, and that I'd fallen in love with Ron. They'd known about my gay lifestyle for a long time by that point, and they knew I'd broken up with Terry. I hoped they'd be happy that I'd found someone else to love who loved me back, and that we were both sober.

I mailed the letter a few days before my mother's March 4 birthday, then Ron and I drove on down to Key West. We rode in a convertible and kept the top down all the way. We stayed in Key West with two of Ron's earlier AIDS buddies, Trip Hoffman and Alan Van Weren. The joke about that was that Ron had such a big personality that he needed two AIDS buddies instead of one. Trip and Alan had done well in real estate back in Virginia and could now afford a beautifully restored house in Key West with a swimming pool in the backyard. They were both lovely guys, and we were happy to be with them.

While in Key West, we happened upon some marine biologists who took us out to chart dolphins on their catamaran. Once we got out on the water, we anchored in an area where dolphins were swimming and diving all around the boat. We were able to get into the water and swim with them. Ron was ecstatic. This all happened by random good luck. We couldn't have planned a better outing.

There was one shadow on the day. On board the catamaran was a 6-year-old girl, Zoe, and she and Ron hit it off immediately. Ron did not, however, hit it off with her stepfather. He had an edge with Zoe that Ron found abusive. Ron was quick to pick up on abuse, possibly because his own father had treated him abusively, and he thought there was something like that going on between Zoe and her stepfather. Until the day he died, whenever we were in church, Ron prayed for Zoe by name during the Prayers of the People. He never let go of his concern for her.

Later on, after we got back from swimming with the dolphins, Ron and I lazed on the porch of our friends' lovely old house. It suddenly registered that it was March 4, and I hadn't yet called my mother for her birthday. I could tell she was happy to hear from me as soon as she picked up her phone.

"Did you get any presents?" I asked.

"Yes," she replied. "I got a present from you."

"But I didn't send you a present; I sent you a letter."

"That's what I'm talking about," she said. "Your letter was the best present of all."

Mom told me that my dad had gone out to the mailbox and returned with her birthday cards. Because mine was addressed to both of them, he'd already read it. When he gave the cards to my mother, he said, "Read this one first. It will make your day." She read it in my father's presence, and the two of them sat there and cried for joy.

It was then that the enormity of my parents' concern for me hit home. They had worried and prayed about me for years. Mom turned 84 on that birthday, and she died three months after turning 86. To this day, I'm grateful that I got sober before my parents died and was able to relieve them of the burden of their distress about my drinking.

There are legendary tales in AA about the efficacy of speaker meetings, and I was privileged to encounter my own legendary speaker, the one with the gravelly voice. I've tried unsuccessfully to find her through the years to thank her for her inspiration. I do my best to express my appreciation for her wise gift in my thoughts and in my prayers.

Ron and I visited Key West a couple more times after that trip. On one of those visits we attended an all-men's meeting at an AA meeting house called Anchors Aweigh. We sat along one side of the room, and when it came time to share, Ron spoke up. He was fearless when it came to speaking his truth. Every now and then, he would get thrown by something, but usually he had no trouble talking about living with AIDS.

That evening, as Ron shared his experience in finding sobriety, he told the room he had AIDS. At that point, the man next to him stood up and left. A few minutes later, he returned and apologized. He said that he had left out of fear but regretted doing so almost immediately afterwards. It was a moment of courage that I've never forgotten, and it meant a lot to both Ron and me.

AA is similar to group therapy in some ways. It's an AA maxim that if you can't be honest and stay honest about your issues, then you can't stay sober. It's understood that repressing the things that trouble you leads back to the bottle. It's essential to talk about them. It takes great courage to acknowledge weakness and fear, and that man found his courage that day. Ron never lost his.

On March 22, 1989 First Lady Barbara Bush took us up on our invitation to visit Grandma's House, the newly established home for children with AIDS. This was a big deal for us and came about after weeks of planning and two meetings at 1600 Pennsylvania Avenue. Distracted by my excitement on the drive to Grandma's House, I made an illegal lane turn right in front of a policeman. He pulled me over on Constitution Avenue, just behind the White House. Puffed up a little by my mission, I offered the excuse that I was about to meet with the First Lady and that my nerves had gotten the better of me. Was he impressed? No, at least not enough to save me from a $75 ticket.

Happily, the rest of the day went exceedingly well. Mrs. Bush arrived promptly on time and joined the circle of those of us representing various AIDS organizations who'd eagerly awaited her arrival. She asked us questions about our work in general and specifically about the residential facility to care for AIDS-infected children at Grandma's House. We shared our experiences and the challenges we faced in our AIDS work, and she listened.

Among those present was Lou Tesconi, the founder of Damien Ministries who himself had AIDS. At one point, Lou said something to the effect of, "You are here to embrace children with AIDS, but I hope you can find it in your heart to embrace all of us who have AIDS." I admired his gumption.

After talking with the adults, Mrs. Bush turned to the children who'd been brought into the room for her to meet. She clearly enjoyed chatting and playing with them. Photographs taken that day reveal her grandmotherly delight, especially while hugging the babies.

As I had my picture taken with her, she turned to me and said playfully, "I don't have to hug you, do I?" I smiled and assured her she didn't. She made sure we all had our photos taken with her individually, and in several group settings. Then we all stepped outside where a bank of TV cameras awaited us, and the First Lady gave a briefing to the press. In concluding her remarks, she turned to Lou Tesconi and said, "I promised this man I'd give him a hug." Whereupon, she turned around and did so. That became the national headline: "First Lady Embraces Man With AIDS."

Mrs. Bush knew exactly what she was doing. She was completely professional, and everything about her seemed genuine and unforced. She won me over that day, and I've been a champion of hers ever since. For years I've proudly displayed one of the group photos taken that day on my office walls. Later, when her son became president, he launched a program to combat AIDS in Africa that has saved millions of lives. I've no doubt that his mother's example influenced his own compassion for those suffering with AIDS.

My family back in Herrin knew about the visit to Grandma's House and watched the news that night in hopes they'd get a glimpse of yours truly. All they saw of me was the arm that reached out to open the First Lady's limousine door. They'd seen her embrace Lou, so they teased me because I didn't get more air time. Beneath the humor, they were deeply grateful that their son did not himself have AIDS.

Those few hours with the wife of the President of the United States were a welcome boost to our morale. We'd spent long, frustrating years ministering to people with AIDS while our government ignored the epidemic. After eight years of silence during the Reagan administration, a compassionate voice had finally been raised and heard at the highest level. It was a euphoric experience.

Terry and I had agreed we'd wait until early 1989 to sell our house in Northern Virginia before going our separate ways. My plan had been to move back into the city, but Ron wanted to stay in Virginia to be near his doctors, home health aides and family members. Terry and his new partner, Chuck Magness, were moving in together, so I bought Chuck's condominium apartment in Arlington. The apartment was spacious with wide picture windows that looked out across the yard onto a nearby wooded area. It was located on the ground floor, so we could step out the door directly into a quiet, private garden.

Ron and I moved in together on April 1st. I left a beautifully decorated miniature Palace of Versailles to move in to a condo with little furniture and not much money to decorate. It was a little shabby, but we were happy.

The day we moved into our new apartment, I was scheduled to officiate at the wedding of Alice Baum and Don Burnes, the

couple who had taken me in and given me work with Samaritan
Ministries after I'd been let go by St. Patrick's. They were the
ones who sat me down and gave me a serious pep talk about
starting an AIDS ministry. Alice was raised Jewish, but I'd baptized her at the National Cathedral several years earlier, and now
she and Don were marrying. I was completely disorganized since
all my clothes were in boxes and ended up wearing pink socks
and cowboy boots. Vestments can cover up a multitude of clerical
idiosyncrasies. Cowboy boots are immensely comfortable, and
I wore them a lot in those years. I was frequently mistaken for a
Texan, especially once the Bushes moved into the White House,
but this Illinois boy just liked cowboy boots. My innovative foot-
wear didn't pass entirely unnoticed on this occasion. Alice later
wrote a poem about her wedding in which she noted the priest
wore pink socks.

That spring was a busy time for AIDS ministries. We'd been
given a boost by the First Lady's visit to Grandma's House, and
the long-awaited AIDS gala being organized by Melody Gilsey
finally had a date: April 7th, 1989. This was the first big gala to get
off the ground, in part because Barbara Bush had come on board
as the honorary chair. It was held at the Sheraton Washington
Hotel, one of the bigger hotels in town, and it hosted a cross section of Washington society.

Around 200 people turned up in black tie to dine and dance
the night away. There wasn't a strong gay presence, but Ron and I
had a lot of fun on the dance floor all the same. Melody told me at
one point, "It feels so good to do this. I'm keeping my promise to
my son that I'd raise money for AIDS."

AIDS was a plague and brought grievous suffering and loss
into the world. At the same time, the epidemic often called forth
the best from people, inspiring their generosity and compassion.
Washington society opened its pocketbook along with its heart at
the gala. Melody and her friends came through for us. Thanks to
them, we had wind in our sails and confidence that we could succeed in our work. Doors were beginning to open.

Even Virginia Seminary, which had banned me from doing
field work with their students at St. Patrick's because I was gay,

seemed to be thawing a little. The day following the gala, Ron and I attended a workshop on AIDS at the seminary. We'd both been invited to serve on a discussion panel at the workshop, something unimaginable only a few years before. It was a small dent in that bastion of conservative resistance, but it was a start. The workshop was arranged by students, not by the administration.

CHAPTER THIRTY

SURRENDER

At last we were making progress, and the ministry was up and running in a way I'd only dreamed of until now. It wasn't long before a harsher reality intruded. The buoyancy of the moment was deflated by Ron's second admission to the hospital for pneumocystis pneumonia, the number one killer of people with AIDS. Ron had been doing fine health-wise; this was his first hospitalization since the summer of 1987. The year before I met Ron, he'd been gravely ill, partly due to his denial about the seriousness of AIDS. He'd ended up in the hospital that time because he'd not been taking good care of himself and had been ignoring the warning signs of his deteriorating condition.

When he left that first hospitalization, he turned over a new leaf, and his health improved dramatically. Now, two years later, the pneumonia was back. Fortunately, he spent only a few days in the hospital this time around. He was about to turn 29 on April 26th, just a week or so away. He came out of the hospital with an IV hook-up attached, full of antibiotics and plans for the future.

Like a number of other gay men who struggled with AIDS, Ron had switched sides politically. "I was determined to be a golden Republican millionaire by the time I was 30," he once confided, "and look at me now, a liberal Democrat." When I first met Ron, he sported a conservative look with dark suits and close-cropped hair. Mind you, he had side-cuts in his hair and a little gold earring in one ear, which hinted at things to come.

Soon after this most recent hospitalization, Ron began visiting a hair design school where he'd spend the entire day getting a low-cost haircut styled to his specifications. Each time he returned home, his hair was cut in a more extreme fashion. It began with just a blond streak, but within a few months he had a full mohawk with purple tints. I just saw it as Ron being Ron, a variation of his skydiving adventure. He knew he was dying and was determined to live what was left of his life fully and on his own terms. He didn't give a damn what anybody else thought. I admit I was a bit shocked by the mohawk, but I grew to love it because I loved Ron. I loved his spirit and all the ways he expressed it.

For Ron's birthday, I wanted to take him back to New York City where we'd had such a fun time the previous fall. I was hell-bent on making it happen, despite the IV needle in Ron's arm and the fact that a home-care nurse was visiting him daily. This is what AA calls "stinking thinking," where the ego takes over and denies the obvious. Even though my intentions were loving, I was denying the reality of the situation and becoming increasingly manic in my attempts to do so.

Among the realities I was ignoring was Big Red. Big Red was Ron's beloved chihuahua, a small yappy dog and a constant reminder of what I'd done for love. Ron's friend Bill Austin raised chihuahuas, and he'd given this one to Ron the previous Christmas. He was red in color and big in spirit; hence, the name. I grew to like him, but he was a one-man dog. He'd sometimes lunge at me when I tried to kiss Ron, and one day he even bit the nurse who'd come to give Ron an infusion.

In a brave moment, I took Big Red along on a trip to the local drugstore to pick up a prescription for Ron. The line at the pharmacy was long and slow. As the minutes passed and the delay continued, I realized that Big Red was still sitting out in the car on a hot day, slowly baking. Even though I'd cracked the windows, I was getting more and more anxious. Ron needed that prescription filled before we could leave for New York, and my stress level rose in proportion to the delay. My back went into spasm, and the pain was killing me. I had to lean on the counter for support.

I was quickly becoming an emotional wreck, but all I could think was, "New York, New York." Then, out of the blue, a familiar inner voice came to my aid. "Say the Serenity Prayer," it whispered. And so, I did just that while leaning against the counter. Peace came almost immediately, and with it came a moment of clarity that bordered on the mystical: Ron didn't care whether or not we went to New York. I knew him well enough to know that he was going to have a good time no matter where he was. Why was I knocking myself out like this? The dam of denial broke, and I was flooded with relief. I acknowledged to myself that we weren't going to make it to New York.

I'm happy to report that Big Red was as feisty as ever when I returned to the car. When I arrived back at our apartment and told Ron I thought it best to skip the New York trip, he said he was perfectly happy to celebrate his birthday at home.

This was a transitional moment for me and a sign that I was beginning to internalize the steps of AA. I was learning about surrender. The Serenity Prayer is powerful in its simplicity: "God grant me the serenity to accept the things I cannot change; courage to change the things I can; and wisdom to know the difference."

Ron knew the Serenity Prayer by heart, and it showed in the optimistic way he lived his life. We had a helium tank on our patio that Ron used to blow up balloons with the slogan: HEAL AIDS WITH LOVE! They were pink and purple and white. We made T-shirts that said the same thing framed inside a big heart. We'd visit friends in the hospital wearing the shirts and carrying a bunch of the balloons.

Many people remained in denial about AIDS and feared the disease with a terror that bordered on superstition.

Onlookers were often thrown by our upbeat display of honesty. I remember one woman who, upon seeing us, claimed with snide defiance, "You can't heal a disease with love!" We weren't the least bit deterred.

Ron Bushnell radiated optimism and light all his life. He was a living shield against negativity. Although Ron was battling a deadly disease, he lightened my darkness and nourished my spirit even in his own darkest hours. I'd been starving all my life for what he gave me. He lifted me up. His optimism and positive approach to life were what attracted me from the beginning.

CHAPTER THIRTY-ONE

BETWEEN HEAVEN
AND HELL

The weekend I'd hoped to spend in New York, Ron and I attended a service at St. Patrick's, my old parish. Jim Steen had invited me to participate in a special service that would celebrate his tenth year as rector. Steve Davenport was still there as the school chaplain, but I'd been gone for four years. I had mixed feelings about accepting the invitation because of the way I'd been let go. I remained conflicted over the whole thing and had been grateful for the excuse of visiting New York instead. But now I figured St. Patrick's was where we were supposed to be.

That particular Sunday was Ron's birthday, and he still had his IV hookup. He sent me on ahead because I was concelebrating with Jim and Steve, and we needed to prepare for the service. Ron hadn't shown up by the beginning of the service, and that made me a little worried. I was relieved to see his big smile when he finally appeared in the back of the church.

There was a big crowd for the service, at least 300 people. An event committee had planned a program to celebrate Jim's and Steve's work, and I'm not sure they even knew I was going to be there. The celebration included the presentation of gifts to Jim and Steve in appreciation for the ways in which they'd served the parish. There was no mention of the work I'd done. The layperson who presided over this part of the service didn't even acknowledge my presence, although I was in clear view, as concelebrant of the Eucharist with Jim and Steve, and had been on the staff several years earlier.

Toward the end of the presentation of the gifts to Jim and Steve, Ron came down the aisle and asked to make a statement. In his big, open-hearted way, he took the microphone and told them that today was his birthday. He said he'd just gotten out of the hospital, and that when he was walking his dog, Big Red, earlier that morning he had said a little prayer to God thanking Him and asking for His blessing.

"Then," he said, "a cardinal lit on a nearby branch and sang me a song, and I knew that God was with me."

Drawing on his enormous courage, he went on to say, "I have AIDS, and I just want to thank St. Patrick's and all the other Episcopal churches that have supported Father Anderson and the Episcopal AIDS Ministry."

You could have heard a pin drop. Jim leaned over and whispered to me: "I think AIDS has just come out of the closet at St. Patrick's." I later found out Steve Davenport was chastised by a parishioner for letting Ron have the microphone.

I'm not sure Ron fully appreciated what his courageous statement meant to me that day. He wasn't all that aware of what had gone on with me and St. Patrick's, because they'd let me go several years before we met. As far as he was concerned, it was simply a time for giving thanks and celebrating the work the church was doing. Ron was a man without guile, and he spoke from the heart. Most of the time, he saw the world from a deeply spiritual perspective as a place of universal interconnection. That made some people nervous. They didn't know how to respond to someone who spoke with such freedom and without fear.

As for me, I was deeply grateful for the way everything worked out for the best. I'd desperately wanted to take Ron to New York for his birthday but had been given this grace-filled moment instead. I'd wanted to give Ron a gift, but he gave one to me, a gift I never could have arranged with all my determination and planning.

Jim was probably right about the importance of Ron's words at St. Patrick's. His public statement made it safer for others to speak. Within a month, one of their choir members was diagnosed with AIDS, and he didn't keep it a secret. If he'd been diagnosed a few months earlier, he might not have felt as free to share the news. AIDS, indeed, had come out of the closet at St. Patrick's.

As 1989 unfolded, there were a lot of funerals to plan, patients to visit in the hospital, and numerous meetings with my board at ECRA, the National Episcopal AIDS Coalition, and other committees. I oversaw volunteer trainings for our group and spoke at various churches about AIDS and our ministry. I continued to conduct healing services at National Cathedral with Carole Crumley.

Attendance at our healing service was sometimes low, but I knew the epidemic was spreading. I suspected people with AIDS might be staying away because of fear of exposure and feelings of intimidation in an imposing setting like the cathedral. I decided to take the ministry to where the people were rather than expecting them to come to the cathedral. On July 13th, Ron and I started our own AIDS healing service at St. Thomas Church near Dupont Circle in a neighborhood with a large gay population. This service was designed specifically for the AIDS community.

The new service was informal and relaxed. We sat in a circle in the lounge of the church, and Ron began the service with a guided meditation. We had a lot of help from Victor Indrosandro, a handsome man with AIDS who was similar to Ron in some ways. He had a warm personality and was irrepressibly outgoing. Victor held a PhD and was on the faculty of a local college. Although confined to a wheelchair because of severe neuropathy, Victor always attended our healing services and contributed to their success. His partner, Matt McGarvey, served as treasurer on the board of my ministry.

The service attracted eight to ten people each week, and we'd often read from "The Color of Light," a book of meditations designed specifically for people with AIDS. We'd read a passage from one of the Gospels, and we'd discuss and reflect upon our readings. It was a welcoming and inclusive group. We made it a safe space where participants could share openly and without fear of judgment.

Over time, many members of our group died from complications of their illness, a heartbreaking experience for those who'd come to know and love them. If there was any comfort to be found in such a situation, it was in the knowledge that we'd done our best to support them while they were alive. Our group helped them overcome the isolation and loneliness that many of them faced in their lives. We gave them a place to be cared for and to be heard.

After services, some of us would regularly head up the street to have lunch at Annie's Paramount Steakhouse, a popular gay bar and restaurant. While the food at Annie's was good, our fellowship was even better. Those Thursday services and our time together afterwards became a mainstay of my spiritual life. We continued to get together every week until I left Washington in 1996.

As a sort of chaplain-at-large to the gay community, I knew that many who came to our services had experienced considerable oppression at the hands of their childhood churches. They wanted spiritual healing, and they wanted to receive it in a loving and accepting environment. We were able to create such a space in all of the venues where we exercised our ministry—the National Cathedral, the Friends Meeting House, on our retreats at the Priest Field Jesuit center, and at St. Thomas' Church. In every case, the sponsoring churches—Episcopal, Protestant and Roman Catholic—were generous in allowing us to welcome people from a mixture of cultures, backgrounds, and beliefs.

We were not there to convert people to Christianity in general or the Episcopal Church in particular. Perhaps in reaction to the heavy-handed proselytizing I'd grown up with in the Pentecostal tradition, I erred on the side of caution in this area. People with AIDS had enough on their plates without having to deal with well-intentioned efforts to save them from Hell. Many of them had already been severely judged most of their lives just for being gay.

As a hospital chaplain, I'd been vigilant in keeping out ministers who put their own needs to save patients from Hell above the patients' needs for compassionate acceptance and love. You cannot baptize the unwilling. It's simply not valid. To convert people was not my goal. I was there to help people with AIDS meet their spiritual needs. I encouraged them to tell their stories and helped them discern their inner wisdom as they told them. In conducting memorial services, I made every effort to ensure that they followed the wishes of the person who had died, even when that differed from what their families wanted.

The last week of September 1989, I was saddened by the news that Bishop Walker had died of heart failure following triple bypass surgery at the age of 64. In a symbolic coincidence, he died as the last stone was laid on the north tower of the cathedral that he was responsible for bringing to completion. The foundation cornerstone had been laid by President Theodore Roosevelt on September 29, 1907, and construction of the National Cathedral continued for decades until President George H.W. Bush laid the final finial stone.

I was in tears. Even though we'd had our differences and our relationship had been a complicated one, I genuinely loved the man. By that time, I'd been in the diocese for fourteen years. I'd recently had a meeting with Bishop Walker and asked if Ron's and my relationship could be blessed in the church. He seemed open to the idea and asked me to write up a service that he could review. I was encouraged to think that my long-time dream of having my relationship blessed in the church might finally become a reality. Distracted by other duties, I didn't get around to submitting a service outline before he died. I am grateful to this day that he listened to my request with an open mind and heart. The bishop's funeral, on October 5, was standing room only.

I was seated with the other clergy of the diocese across from President and Mrs. Bush, who had a place of honor. It was a magnificent service with glorious music: "Fanfare for the Common Man" by Aaron Copland, and a gospel song, "When I Die Give Me Jesus," sung by a black woman with an outstanding voice.

In October, Ron and I flew to Cincinnati, Ohio, to take part in the first National Episcopal AIDS Conference. It took place over a weekend, offered workshops and keynote speakers, and included a healing service. It was a gathering of several hundred people with AIDS and people like me from across the country who were engaged in AIDS ministries. It was actually an extension of the group we'd formed in San Francisco in 1988 but on a much larger scale. It was a spirited event with enthusiastic participants and felt like a cross between a regular convention and an old-fashioned revival.

The airport serving Cincinnati is actually just over the state line in Kentucky, so we had to cross the Ohio River to get to our destination. The Ohio River flows southwest from Cincinnati to the Mississippi River and forms the southeastern boundary of the state of Illinois. Before the Civil War, the Ohio River also marked the boundary between slave states and free states.

My hometown of Herrin is located midway between the Ohio and Mississippi Rivers. Even though I was born 75 years after the Civil War, I was aware even as a child of how close we were to the former slave states. I knew that the Underground Railroad had smuggled slaves across the Ohio River to the north and that there had been a kind of reverse railroad, a slave house in Southern Illinois whose owner kidnapped freed slaves and captured escaping slaves to sell them back south. As Ron and I drove across the Ohio River into Cincinnati, I felt we were members of another oppressed minority crossing that river in hopes of gaining our freedom.

We'd made progress at the Episcopal General Convention the previous summer, but our gains were tenuous. During the AIDS conference in Cincinnati, we held our services at Christ Church Cathedral. The week after we left, we read in a news article that some of the cathedral's regular parishioners were outraged that "all those people with AIDS" had been in their cathedral—so much so that they walked about sprinkling holy water to purify their sacred space. That's the kind of fear and ignorance that continued to afflict some people as the first decade of the epidemic drew to a close.

CHAPTER THIRTY-TWO

A Visit to Herrin

That Thanksgiving, Ron and I flew to Herrin, where he was warmly welcomed by my parents. Although people in Herrin were somewhat shocked at how open I was in the 1970s and '80s, my parents had always been supportive. I took their stability, love, and support for granted as a child. I didn't realize until much later in life just how lucky I'd been to grow up in such a family. Despite my uncomfortable awareness that I was different from other boys, I always felt accepted at home.

I was excited to introduce Ron to my parents and to my hometown. They knew he had AIDS and welcomed him with open arms. In what seemed like no time at all, my parents fell in love with him. As I washed dishes in the kitchen with my mother, we listened to Ron and my father talking spiritual talk in the next room like two old wise men. Ron returned with me twice more to visit Herrin and my parents in the time we had left.

As 1989 drew to a close, we were riding high. I had a year of sobriety under my belt and felt energized and supported in my work as an AIDS chaplain. I was in demand as a speaker, and our retreats for people with AIDS were going strong. Episcopal congregations responded increasingly with respect and compassion to my attempts at consciousness-raising about AIDS.

Ron and I were invited to speak to a group of about 400 high school boys during a service at Washington's prestigious St. Alban's School and to another large group of students at Episcopal High School in Alexandria, Virginia. Lou Tesconi of Damien Ministries and I even spoke at the Navy's Washington, D.C. headquarters to an assembly of Naval officers and were well received. Ron continued to be involved with his AA work and contributed to our men's AIDS retreats whenever he could.

Change was in the air. AIDS was no longer a hidden disease but a publicly recognized epidemic to be openly battled with public and private funding, focused medical research, and compassion.

CHAPTER THIRTY-THREE

1990

Looking back, I remember 1990 as the year I reclaimed my spiritual power. I'd spent years as a gay man trying to make a life for myself in my country and in my church while pretending to be someone else. Ours was indeed a love that dared not speak its name. When AIDS began attacking gay men, we became a target for even greater fear and judgment. Every day was a battle against shame and oppression. And yet, in its vulnerability, the gay community rallied and found a powerful voice in its struggle to survive. Many of us finally realized we'd tolerated ignorance and discrimination long enough. In caring for one another while many in the broader culture were content to let us die, we discovered we were no longer willing to live as victims.

By 1990, over 100,000 Americans had died of AIDS. In that year alone, I was involved in twenty-eight funerals or memorial services, over forty healing services, and had made 110 hospital visits to people with AIDS. We held three AIDS retreats and performed one baptism.

Ron was my friend, my lover, and my mentor throughout. With him by my side, I took back my spiritual power from the culture to which I'd ceded it for most of my life. I didn't know it then, but the events of 1990 were to change my life forever. Ron was like a spiritual rocket booster that propelled me into the heavens and another level of spiritual awareness altogether. When my booster fell away, I kept soaring.

My father and I had seldom discussed spiritual matters, but he did so readily with Ron. During one of our visits, he suggested than Ron and I read the Epistle of James from the New Testament. We did so not long afterwards. In early 1990, Ron and I attended an AA men's retreat at a Jesuit retreat house on the Potomac River in Maryland. The retreat center is located at a pleasant spot just where the river widens. There, lying on the grass along the bank of the river, we read the Epistle of James together. I felt deeply connected to my father as Ron and I read aloud the author's wise advice. This epistle counsels perseverance and patience during times of trial and is the chief biblical text supporting anointing of the sick. Clearly, this was the text that had given my father a biblical basis to support our AIDS ministry of healing. Had it not been for Dad's connection with Ron, I may never have come to this moment of understanding. We felt his love there beside us.

Another moment stands out from that retreat. Ron was usually able to stay optimistic and positive as we walked through the epidemic, as evidenced by his Heal AIDS with Love motto on T-shirts and balloons. Every now and then, though, something or someone would puncture a balloon. That AA retreat marked one such occasion.

We celebrated the final evening of the retreat with an ice cream social. Ron was always front and center when it came time for a party, and this time he volunteered to help scoop and serve the ice cream. We had attended several of these AA retreats together and knew quite a few of the other men who were there. They accepted us as a gay couple and knew Ron had AIDS, so we felt comfortable and safe as the party got underway.

I was outside eating my ice cream and talking with someone when Ron walked out of the dining hall with his tail between his legs. Another ice cream server had said to him, "I don't think you should be handling the ice cream," and the comment wounded Ron to the quick. He'd been made to feel unclean.

I was furious and said, "Ron Bushnell, you get back in there and start dipping ice cream right now." For good measure, I added, "I think that guy is gay and closeted. He should know better." Ron gave me a smile, stiffened his back, and walked back to return to his serving duties. It was a reminder that although we'd made progress, we still had a way to go in educating people about this disease. I wanted to strangle the other guy and wonder if I would have if Ron hadn't recovered his equilibrium.

The 1990 Washington Diocesan Convention was held in January at the National Cathedral, and I was invited to participate in a panel discussion with David Scott, a professor of Christian ethics at the Episcopal seminary in Alexandria. Dr. Scott was a strong supporter of the seminary's policy statement opposing the ordination of "active and or advocating" homosexuals to the priesthood of the Episcopal Church. He'd been part of the group that banned me from supervising field work with student seminarians when I served on the staff of St. Patrick's Church.

The panel was moderated by NPR radio host Diane Rehm, and it was the first time anybody could recall public mention of homosexuality in the cathedral. The news media were on hand to report the event. There would be a lot of people watching, and for better or worse, the way I comported myself could reflect on the gay community more generally. I needed to calm my nerves and spent a few minutes before the debate saying my prayers in the Holy Spirit Chapel.

Any number of the other gay clergy present could have expressed themselves more eloquently than I did, but I didn't embarrass myself. Dr. Scott warned the convention that affirming homosexual behavior would violate biblical teachings. "The Genesis accounts of creation say to me that God's will for human sexual relating is heterosexual," he said. I countered that similar appeals to scripture had been used to justify any number of beliefs now understood to be wrong, including sexism and slavery. I talked about the kinds of discrimination gay people faced in every avenue of life and urged the church not to perpetuate them. I mentioned the Seminary's ban on my supervision of its students as an example. I observed that the church was becoming more open to gay people and their concerns and that an invitation for a gay priest to debate a professor of Christian ethics in the National Cathedral was a sign of progress.

The question-and-answer period following our discussion was memorable for one contribution in particular. A woman from a conservative charismatic Episcopal church expressed her condemnation of homosexuals who dared love each other by shouting out: "Sodomy!" The word echoed through the nave for a long time.

It's not surprising that traditionalists were uncomfortable with my remarks. I'd argued that the love between two men or

two women could as easily be an avenue to God as the love between a man and a woman, that my love for my partner Ron had
brought me closer to God. Clearly, my statements ran against the
grain of centuries of tradition that had condemned such a possibility out of hand.

News of the debate made it all the way back to my hometown
of Herrin. One of the local residents by the name of Joyce came
across an article about our panel discussion in The Living Church,
a news magazine read in many Episcopal parishes across the
country. Joyce and her husband were movers and shakers in the
Diocese of Springfield where I'd first joined the Episcopal Church.
Joyce brought the article to her Women's Club luncheon where
her criticism of my remarks sparked another lively debate.

It so happens that my high school English literature teacher,
Miss Ruth Sullivan, was at the luncheon. As soon as Joyce began
putting me down, Miss Sullivan loudly proclaimed, "Jerry was
one of my best-ever students. I don't know what he's up to now,
but whatever it is, I'm sure it's okay," bringing further criticism of
yours truly to an abrupt close.

I loved Miss Sullivan. I can still remember her tapping out the
rhythm of Shakespearian iambic pentameter on her desk with a
ruler. I rather like the image of her smacking down her ruler years
later on my behalf. Her introduction of Elizabethan literature gave
me a foretaste of the Episcopal Book of Common Prayer, which
was a product of the same period in English literature. I came to
love the Prayer Book.

Meanwhile, my ministry was expanding, and we needed
more room than the Carl Vogel Foundation could provide. The
National Episcopal AIDS Coalition decided around that time to
locate its headquarters in downtown Washington, D.C., and we
at ECRA joined them in renting a common space. Our new offices
were located only a block and a half from the White House in an
old office building at 15th and H Streets. Our two organizations
agreed to share an office manager, and we hired one of the ECRA
board members to serve in that capacity.

CHAPTER THIRTY-FOUR

SAMOA

A month after my debate with David Scott, Ron was diagnosed with Mycobacterium Avium-Intracellulare Infection or MAI, one of the opportunistic infections to which people with AIDS are especially susceptible because of their compromised immune systems. The bacteria that cause MAI are present in drinking water and don't pose a threat to people with fully functioning immune systems. For people like Ron, however, MAI could be deadly.

Although Ron's doctors were able to bring his MAI infection under control fairly quickly, this episode got his attention. It was a reminder that he didn't have forever to do all the things he wanted to do in his lifetime. Ron's mother, Lida, was from a prominent family in American Samoa, and Ron had always wanted to visit there.

Ron had seen something of the world beyond the U.S. as a teenager. His father, Robert, was from Nebraska, and the family had spent time in Kuwait when Robert worked for the State Department. They'd never visited Samoa as a family, though, and Ron was determined to do so before he died.

Ron's mother had other ideas. She was a feisty, strong-willed force of nature, and she did not want her son showing up in Samoa. She argued that Samoa had poor medical facilities and that Ron would be in grave peril if he got sick while visiting. Ron believed this was just a smoke screen to cover up the real reason for her opposition: Her son was gay and had AIDS, and when the news got out in Samoa, it would scandalize the family.

Lida claimed Samoan royal heritage and that the King of Tonga was her cousin. She would tell anyone who would listen that her family had given Samoa to the American government. Her brother, Peter Coleman, was the Governor of Samoa, and the family counted many friends among those serving in the Samoan diplomatic community. They were Republicans, and many of them drank a lot.

Lida had spent a lot of time in Samoa over the years, involving herself in her brother's political campaigns and other elements of island life. She milked her political and social connections for all they were worth as she launched a major campaign to keep us from visiting. She had her relatives call from Samoa to dissuade Ron from going. She even had a gay cousin in Hawaii urge Ron not to go.

Ron had inherited his mother's larger-than-life personality. He felt he'd been denied his Samoan heritage long enough, and nothing was going to keep him away now. The battle raged for two weeks as Ron and his mom got into loud arguments. Neither of them did things by halves. There was no chance of our slipping onto the island unnoticed, so we had to do so publicly and hang the consequences. Naturally, as Ron's lover and champion, I shared his determination.

We left for Samoa on April 1st, 1990 with a stopover in Honolulu to visit Father Jack Harris, the close friend and priest who had baptized me in the Episcopal Church many years before. Later, he'd been rector of the church in San Francisco where the common chalice was banned from the communion service due to fear of AIDS. My visit with him in 1983 had been my first encounter with the effects of the disease and marked the beginning of my involvement in the AIDS crisis.

While we were in Honolulu, Lida played her ace card. Ron's uncle, the Governor of Samoa, called us at Jack's vacation condo. Ron took the call and listened quietly for a few minutes before saying, "Uncle Pete, I'm not going to give anybody AIDS in Samoa. I only have sex with my lover." Covering the mouthpiece of the phone with his hand, he turned to me and said, "He's going to arrest us if we come to Samoa."

By this time, I'd had enough. We'd been fighting off Ron's mother for two weeks, and now her brother had joined the fray.

"Give me the phone!" I demanded.

I'd seen Uncle Pete in action, and I had his measure. He was a Republican crony and had palled around with Vice President

Dan Quail when Quail made a few of his infamous public gaffs. I wasn't about to be intimidated. I grabbed that receiver, introduced myself, and exaggerated: "I have as much political influence at the White House as you do!" I then informed him, truthfully, that Ron's doctor had okayed Ron's health and signed off on the trip. I told the Governor of Samoa that he was ignorant and that he needed to get himself educated about AIDS and how it was transmitted. I was actually shouting by that point. Then Uncle Pete put his daughter, Ron's cousin, on the phone, and I started yelling at her. The conversation didn't end well.

We had tickets to board the plane to Samoa the next day. "Dear Lord, what's going to happen?" I thought. I'd never flown halfway around the world before, so I had no idea what to expect. "Could they do that—arrest tourists for having AIDS?" I wondered.

Honolulu Airport was in chaos when we arrived, thronged with Samoans heading home from Hawaii. We finally made it to the ticket agent, an attractive young woman in her twenties, and she asked us for our passports. "Passports?" I asked. "Isn't American Samoa in America?" We had no passports. Why did we need passports?

"Because it would be easy for travelers to slip onto one of the other islands, we need your passports," she explained. "Goddammit!" I thought. If Ron's family had been more cooperative, we'd have known about this sort of thing. We'd gone through Hell to get this far, and now we were being turned back at the final gate. I was rapidly approaching the end of my tether.

Then came Ron to the rescue. In his typical charming fashion, he told her, "Oh, call the Governor, he's my uncle." I thought he'd gone nuts. His uncle had promised to arrest us the first chance he got, so I couldn't see what good calling him would do. But this pretty young woman said, "Oh, you mean Uncle Pete?" Ron said, "Yes, is he your uncle, too?"

She disappeared behind a partition. The way things were going, I was about to tear my hair out. Then she returned. The plane was boarding, and—I must have been dreaming—she escorted us on board, leading us to the front of the plane where she asked a large Samoan man to give up his seat, so Ron and I could sit together in First Class. Well, sort of First Class. It was surreal, and she managed it with that lovely, gentle grace people from

South Pacific cultures so often embody. Soon, we were soaring high above the equator toward Ron's ancestral homeland.

My euphoric relief at getting on the flight was short-lived. I was wound up over what to expect once we landed. The trip seemed to go on forever. We took off in daylight and soon entered what seemed to be an endless night. It was black as ink, so we couldn't see anything out the window. I must have been asleep when the pilot announced the descent into Pago Pago, because when we hit the runway I thought we'd crashed. The plane just seemed to go Ka-rruumph! onto the tarmac. Everyone else seemed unfazed, so I tried to calm down.

American Samoa is not much larger than the District of Columbia. Given its small size and tiny population, there would be no place to run from the governor. When we got off the plane in Pago Pago, I looked around for the police who were coming to arrest us, but they were nowhere to be seen. Mercifully, it seemed the governor's threats had been empty, and we were free to enjoy our visit.

We caught a cab to our hotel, which was supposedly the best on the island. It came complete with a cushion of moss clinging to the walls of our shower, and a swimming pool tinted an algae green. The place was no Ritz Carlton, but it was better than a jail cell.

Samoa reminded me of the Hawaiian Islands with its lush foliage, gorgeous beaches, and mountains. We could see the governor's big white mansion up on the side of a mountain not far from our hotel. That first morning, I kept waiting for the governor to call or the police to find and arrest us, but they never did. We decided we might feel more at home if we attended an AA meeting, so off we went.

It was a small group, and we met a very friendly Canadian couple. They were both doctors on a sailing trip around the world and had stopped in Samoa to work at the local health clinic for a few weeks. Later, when I saw the Lyndon Johnson Health Clinic—Samoa's answer to a hospital and primitive by mainland standards—I couldn't help but think, "No wonder Lida was concerned."

We also met a gay man who was living in Samoa, and he invited us to dinner. That's where we learned about Samoa's fa'afafines. To the western ear, the word sounds like "fa fa feenies," and translated means, "in the manner of a woman."

Considered to belong to a third gender in the Samoan tradition, the fa'afafines are people assigned male gender at birth who embody both male and female behavioral traits into adulthood. Samoan society is tolerant of differences and doesn't force its children to conform to strict gender roles as is common in most western countries. I was reminded of how accepting my parents had been of my own feminine identifications as a child.

We got to meet some members of the fa'afafines community when the woman doctor we'd met at the AA meeting took us on a tour of the island. We stopped for lunch at a tourist site, and our servers were fa'afafines. Although they had painted fingernails and wore colorful clothes in a style we thought of as feminine, they were not at all like American transvestites or transgender persons. They were a separate entity in and of themselves and were clearly accepted by and at home in their culture.

After lunch, our new doctor friend asked to stop by the house of a local woman who had completed some sewing for her. We arrived to find the seamstress in the middle of making a wedding dress for her younger daughter. Upon learning the family was Mormon, Ron asked, "Do you know my cousin Rose? She's Mormon."

"Oh!" replied the seamstress, "Rose is your cousin? We go to the same church. Does she know you're here?" When Ron replied that she did not, the seamstress said, "Well, I'll call her!"

From that moment on, the Mormon side of Ron's family welcomed us with open arms. We felt we'd entered the Promised Land where grace abounded. They gave us their pick-up truck, and we drove around the island and swam in the Pacific Ocean. They introduced us to village life. Each family compound featured an open-air meeting house with a thatched roof where the family gathered and sometimes slept. There was lots of singing, and music filled the air everywhere we went in the four days we were there.

On Sunday morning, we stopped by the Roman Catholic church, but it was so boring we left. We could hear the 60-voice choir of the much larger Congregational Church down the road, so we went there instead. The minister greeted us warmly at the door, and I told him where we were from and a little about my work. During the service, he prayed a beautiful prayer for Ron and me and for my ministry.

At the end of the service, an attractive woman in the pew in front of us turned around and said, "I have a TV show here, and I'd like to do a live interview with you about your ministry." Regrettably, we were scheduled to leave at 4 o'clock the next morning, so it didn't happen. There's no doubt that if we had appeared on the TV show, Ron would have told the woman he had AIDS, thereby sparing his mother the trouble of any further efforts to keep her son's illness a secret.

News of Ron's visit had almost certainly gotten around the island in record time. Everywhere we went, Ron would ask, "Do you know Lida Bushnell?" Almost everyone did, and Ron would let them know she was his mother.

The warm welcome we received from Ron's Mormon family lifted our hearts after weeks of having been urged not to come by his Roman Catholic relatives. The governor hadn't followed through on his threat to have us arrested, but we were told he had a drinking problem. Everybody knew his chauffeur regularly had to pour him back into his limo after social events. The Mormons, by contrast, didn't drink and they treated us like the visiting royalty Ron's mother claimed to be.

That Sunday afternoon after the church service, cousin Rose and her family cooked up a big feast in our honor. The windows of their house were thrown wide open, letting the sea breezes come through to caress our bodies and souls. Pigs and chickens were running around outside, squealing and clucking, as though to remind us that we were in a very different place from where we'd come. Several more of Ron's cousins turned up along with an old woman who had helped raise Lida many years before.

Before dinner, Ron's cousin's husband gathered us all together and, as was their custom, asked that we kneel in prayer to give thanks. We all knelt on the floor, and he prayed a most beautiful prayer. As I listened to him pray, I wept and thanked God for bringing us to this moment. We'd been through hell to get there, but Ron was clearly in heaven. He'd made it to his mother's homeland, and he'd been enveloped by the love of some of the members of his family.

CHAPTER THIRTY-FIVE

A GREAT LOSS

Ron was beginning to slow down. We stopped in Honolulu on the way home and stayed with Jack Harris for another few days. Ron and I had been planning a trip to England in August, but when Jack heard this, he took me aside and said softly, "Jerry, I don't think Ron will be up for going to England." What was obvious to Jack had not been obvious to me. I'd been in denial about Ron's health for some time. Ron was the most positive person I'd ever known. How could he not beat AIDS? It took Jack to point out that Ron was walking more slowly and had far less stamina.

I was not in denial, however, about Samoa's boost to Ron's morale. Seeing him so happy did my heart good as well. Only later did I realize that fulfilling Ron's longstanding dream of a sojourn in the South Pacific had also given him permission to begin letting go.

Although I'd known and loved Jack for years, his observation that Ron wasn't well enough to go to England left me bristling. For almost a year, Ron had been keeping pace with my hectic schedule without any trouble. But now neuropathy was setting in, and he was having trouble walking without a cane. I contemplated our future with sorrow but not with dread. Somehow it wasn't sinking in that he'd be gone one day. Perhaps one day soon.

Summer arrived early that year, and several things happened in June that kept up our spirits. The first was that our ECRA ministry team marched in the Gay Pride Parade in the nation's capital. Thousands of enthusiastic people turned out for the event, and it was exhilarating. Ron and I hosted a cook-out in the back yard of our condo for 28 people that week. We had a bishop, several priests, two gay millionaires, and several people with AIDS.

Our modest apartment was nothing like the luxurious showplace where I'd once entertained guests with Terry, and it didn't matter. Everyone had fun, and the evening was a great success.

Later that summer, we celebrated our first gay wedding at the Friends Meeting House. The Episcopal Church was years away from blessing gay marriage, and the Quakers hadn't yet decided whether they would do so. When I asked the D.C. Quaker community if we could use their meeting space, they held a meeting to discuss the matter. Although they didn't come to a consensus about whether to permit gay marriage for Quakers, they did decide to allow someone who was not a Quaker to use their meeting house for that purpose. Once again, we were breaking barriers and forging ahead.

I had quietly blessed a gay union between two friends who were Episcopal priests fifteen years earlier in a private setting, and that was the only time I'd officiated at such an event. Now such occasions were becoming more common and more public. Our first gay wedding in the Quaker Meeting House was announced in the newspapers and celebrated the union of a popular couple who'd been active in the Washington gay community: Mario Montoya, a well-known lawyer who worked at the Whitman-Walker Clinic, and his partner, Christopher Echols. Two hundred people attended the service, including two candidates running in that year's D.C. mayoral race.

The Washington Blade, our local gay newspaper, ran a feature article on the event and included a large photo of the happy couple with me in the background. Although this was one of the first public blessings of a gay union, there was no official license. The union had no legal status. That the U.S. Supreme Court would someday declare that gay people had a constitutional right to marry was all but inconceivable. But that didn't stand in the way of high spirits at the grand reception following the service. There was a DJ and music with dancing around a large outdoor swimming pool. Ron danced in his wheelchair, moving artfully to and fro with the music. Despite his infirmities, nothing got in the way of his enjoyment of the moment. It was an altogether magnificent day.

On July 3, I returned home to Herrin for my 30th high school reunion. Ron had not been feeling well and decided to stay home. I was worried about him so made it a quick trip. I did have time to see Mary Heard Wallace who'd been a close friend when we were in high school. She was working as a nurse with AIDS patients in Seattle. Mary and her care team had produced a video about their work that won first prize at the World AIDS Conference in Toronto. All these years later, we served a common cause.

Mary expressed concern that I didn't seem like my old self. It was true. In past years I'd stood front and center in the group photo taken of our class reunion. That year, I was off to one side in my own world.

Ron's condition deteriorated in July, and he was admitted to the hospital for five days to receive a series of injections and special care. When I brought him home on a Friday afternoon, he was his usual upbeat self. After helping him settle in and taking a nap together, I headed into town because some overzealous members of our board had called a meeting on a Friday night. I got up and left while Ron remained in bed sleeping.

When I arrived home later that night, I found Ron absolutely hysterical, sobbing on the phone to his sister, Marsha. I'd told him where I was going, but when he woke up alone, he was convinced I'd abandoned him. I'd never seen him that way before, and I never saw him like that again.

Ron had been seeing a therapist, so we decided I'd go with him to a few sessions. His father, Robert, was a bullying homophobe who'd never accepted Ron. In therapy, it emerged that Ron believed I was pulling away from him, just as his father had done. In that moment, I knew what had to be said. "I am not leaving you, Ron," I promised. "You're the one who's leaving me." That gave Ron the clarity he needed to let go of his fear—even as it reminded me of my own great loss still to come.

Although it was clear Ron was in no shape to go to England as we'd hoped, he encouraged me to make the trip on my own. I didn't want to do it without him, but I needed a break, and I suspected Ron needed one, too. We corralled at least ten friends and arranged for a different one to do something with Ron each day that I'd be gone.

Once in England, I reached out to other priests involved in AIDS ministry, including a former professor from my seminary years in Manhattan. In London, I met with Father Bill Kirkpatrick, a priest who'd been working for years with the gay community and had been among the first to visit and to bury AIDS patients when others were afraid to do so in the early years of the epidemic. Together we visited The Lighthouse, the well-known AIDS care center whose patients were frequently visited by Princess Diana.

I took the train up to Sheffield, where the liturgical poet and priest Jim Cotter had a small retreat house. Jim was one of the first priests in England to come out publicly. He had done this in the 1970s and written about it extensively. He had known brokenness and suffering in his own life and was a healing presence to others seeking wholeness.

I traveled on to Wales and spent time with Father Donald Allchin, a former seminary professor of mine in New York. Donald was vivacious, fun and quite demonstrative for an Englishman. We had a splendid time driving around Wales and enjoying the countryside. Along the way, we celebrated mass in a small church that had been built in the 5th century. This wasn't our first trip together. In the spring of 1968, Donald had invited me to visit with him the Trappist monk Thomas Merton at the Abbey of Gethsemani in Kentucky. We spent the day with Merton visiting his friends in Lexington. This happened to be April 4, and later in the day we learned that Martin Luther King, Jr. had been assassinated in Memphis. Merton wrote in detail about this day in his diary. Later that year he died in Thailand.

After my time in Wales, I headed off to Cambridge University where I had lunch with Norman Pittenger, another professor from my seminary years in Manhattan and one of the first theologians to call for full acceptance of homosexual relationships. Norman had been the keynote speaker at the first Episcopal gay conference in Chicago in 1975, and I had been one of the gay priests who concelebrated the Eucharist at the conference. It was a daring stance to take, but by 1975 I was determined to be out of the closet.

When I was in seminary back in 1966, Norman had preached a sermon during which he quoted from Giovanni's Room, a book by James Baldwin which has as a central theme the exploration of sexual identity and love. It was springtime in New York, and I was falling in love all over the place. To hear one of my professors preaching affirmatively about such a topic at that time in that place had been a life-changing experience.

The trip to England renewed my spirit and gave me a helpful perspective on the work I'd been doing for nearly a decade. It was good for my soul, and I was grateful.

When I arrived home from the airport, Ron welcomed me with a lovely filet mignon dinner he'd cooked with the help of a friend. He'd also bought me a piece of jewelry as a gift. It was a pinkie ring with a black onyx stone. It was wonderful to be together again, and we enjoyed jubilant high spirits which would not last much longer. All too soon, we found ourselves in a downward spiral.

Jack Harris came for a visit in late August, and Ron and I took him to dinner at Annie's Paramount Steakhouse in the largely gay DuPont Circle neighborhood. We took a booth at the back of the restaurant. Ron loved eating out and was having a great time. Just before dessert Ron swallowed a handful of the pills he had to take every evening with meals. Then he said, "Uh oh, I don't feel too good." With the help of his walking cane, he got up and headed to the bathroom. Before he could make it, he threw up, slid on his vomit and fell down. I lifted him up off the floor and took him into the bathroom, where he finished throwing up. I cleaned him up as best as I could, but he was utterly mortified.

When we came out of the bathroom, he apologized to everyone, and people couldn't have been nicer. We got in the car to go home, and Ron began sobbing. He cried and cried all the way home.

Once we were back inside our apartment, he said, "When you picked me up off the floor, you were saying, 'Oh Ron, oh Ron.'" I didn't remember that I'd said anything at all. "I felt such a strong sense of compassion from you," Ron continued, "that I knew then for sure you'd never desert me."

I realized that even with all the therapy we'd done, Ron had continued to struggle with fears of abandonment. As difficult as that evening was, Ron's acceptance of my support and love was a powerful gift for us both and one I've rarely shared. He never feared my abandoning him after that.

Several days later, I took Ron to see our last movie together. It was the Bette Midler film Beaches that ends with her singing Wind Beneath My Wings, the beautiful tribute to her dying friend. We were both in tears. It was such an emotionally loaded time for us and for so many others losing loved ones to AIDS. How could you not sob?

The next ECRA AIDS retreat was scheduled for September, and although he could barely walk by that point, Ron was there. Before we left, he asked me to bring along a sheet and a floodlight for his part in the talent show portion of our gathering. When his turn came to perform, Ron stood between the floodlight and the sheet so that the audience saw only his silhouette. As Bette Midler's voice sang Wind Beneath My Wings from a CD player, Ron gracefully moved his arms to interpret the lyrics of the song. It seemed that nothing could kill his spirit.

Events were moving swiftly now. Not long after the retreat, Ron's close friend Bill Austin died. He'd been deteriorating at the same rate as Ron. We went over to Bill's house and shared our tears with his long term partner, Robert Gray, and two other close friends. The following Sunday, we took part in the annual AIDS walk which had become a major fundraiser in the nation' capital. Ron was in a wheelchair and had great fun as we pushed him along with the rest of us. His nieces Lisa and Julia came with their mother Marsha. You'd have thought Ron was Queen of the May, he enjoyed it so much. But that was Ron's—for lack of a better phrase—last public appearance.

A week later, on Saturday the 30th of September, I officiated at a gay wedding at the Friends Meeting House where the bride and one of the bridesmaids were dressed in drag. The next day Ron's good friend Tony Head died. Tony and Ron had gotten to know each other during the AIDS Mastery program led by Sally Fischer. Tony was a natural mime who could do a convincing Barbara Bush in drag. We held his memorial service at the Friends Meeting House on October 2. The next day, Ron was admitted to the hospital.

When Ron was living as a teenager in Kuwait, he'd gone diving in the Arabian Sea with a boyfriend. His friend brought up a piece of black coral which he gave to Ron as a token of his affection. Ron had the coral capped with gold and mounted on a chain and had worn it constantly ever since. As we were getting ready to leave for the hospital, I was on the phone to Ron's sister when he took the coral necklace from around his neck and put it around mine. When I mentioned what he'd done to Marsha, she responded, "This makes me feel uneasy. Do you think he's trying to tell you something?"

I asked Ron if he were giving me the necklace for safekeeping or because he thought he'd never wear it again. "For safekeeping," he optimistically replied.

The AIDS Quilt returned to the Washington Mall on October 7 that year, and once again ECRA had planned an interfaith healing service at the National Cathedral to mark the occasion. The newly elected Bishop, Ron Haines, who'd taken Bishop Walker's place, was much more supportive, so we didn't have to fight the old battles again. The Gay Men's Chorus attended, and this time sang a solo anthem without controversy. I managed to have Larry Uhrig invited to be the preacher. Larry was well known for founding the Washington, D.C. branch of the Metropolitan Community Church, a fellowship with special outreach to the gay and lesbian community. Nobody objected to the invitation. Larry had seen his share of discrimination. He was fine preacher and proved to be an inspired choice.

Ron was in the Washington Hospital Center, a major medical facility located directly east of the cathedral. I'd visited him there every day since his hospitalization while going about my other duties. His window faced west, so we could see the cathedral high above the city on Mount St. Alban and the sunsets beyond.

One evening, I said to Ron, "Remember that when we worship at the AIDS healing services at the cathedral we face east in this direction. All that healing power is headed right toward you." Although Ron could no longer attend the services in person, we were always joined on those occasions in spirit.

As Ron continued to decline, I spent most of my available hours camped out in his room. I'd sometimes lie carefully on the bed next to him and hold his hand while we watched television or just talked. I soon found out from Betsy Findley—one of the hospital nurses who was also on our board at the AIDS ministry—that the head nurse was upset that I was "in bed" with Ron. Betsy asked her if she'd be upset if we were a heterosexual couple."

"Yes," she said. "It's inappropriate." Ron couldn't resist telling some wicked Nurse Ratched jokes in his usual good humor.

The nurse never said anything to Ron or to me, and we continued to be physically close and affectionate. It's remarkable how often people in the healing professions don't understand the importance of giving and receiving physical comfort at such times. Touch is healing. Closeness is what we seek for most of our lives. It seems cruel to withhold it when it's so easy to give, especially to loved ones when they are seriously ill.

We were grateful to the nursing staff for their compassion and care. On one occasion, however, they were overwhelmed with work, and I responded with uncharacteristic anger. Ron underwent a procedure to drain his lungs and was restricted from drinking any liquids for several hours. He was parched by the end of that time, but nobody came by with any water. I walked down to ask the duty staff for help, and still the water didn't come. It took me about twenty minutes to lose my patience. Due to my many visits, I knew the hospital well, so I entered a "Nurses Only" kitchenette to get the water for Ron myself. This was the only unit that had such a restriction. As I was leaving, one of the nurses blocked me in to scold me. Well, I lost it. I really let her have it. Ron told me later that he could hear me all the way down in his room. I stormed past the nurse and charged on down the corridor with the water. I was fed up.

And I was worried about Ron.

On one visit, as I was lying on the bed next to Ron, he wanted to know if I'd date anyone else after he died. "What do you think?" I asked. "Would it bother you?" He looked at me and smiled. "They're going to have to be pretty special, aren't they?" This was more of Ron's playful spirit at work, and it was both a blessing and a curse. His words haunted me for a long time because he was right. I doubt he fully grasped the lasting impact he'd have on my life. Neither did I, until later. We lived very much in the present.

My life became a blur as I tried to meet the demands of my schedule and visit Ron at the hospital every day. I'm not sure how I made it through. My friends expressed their love and concern in many ways. One friend, Don Chamblee, mixed me an audio cassette tape of beautiful music that I played over and over in the Supra as I drove from place to place. Bob Alfandre gave many of us a boost by hosting a Halloween costume party. The invitation stated that we'd had enough funerals; it was time to have some fun. I didn't want to go without Ron, but he insisted, and so I did—in drag!

I looked fabulous if I do say so myself, but I had a lot of help. A priest friend did my makeup and Steve Lembesis, our ECRA board president, loaned me a pink dress and a blonde wig. I became "Connie from Arlington." I'd forgotten to get gas in the rush of getting ready, so I had to stop at a service station on the drive through town to the party. I stood there in my high heel shoes and pink chiffon outfit, pumping gas while the cold October wind blew up my dress and drivers did double-takes from the cars passing by on the street.

I stopped by the hospital, so Ron could see me in costume. The hospital staff had only ever seen me as a priest, and I created quite a sensation as I walked down the halls. Ron loved "Connie" and was happy to send me off to the party in style. When I left the hospital, I decided to take a less conspicuous route that led past the chaplain's office. The door was open and standing just inside were a Roman Catholic priest and Dixie Bosley, a social worker who was on our retreat staff. I stuck my head in and said, "Hi." Dixie couldn't believe her eyes. We laughed, and the priest took pictures. We didn't have Facebook then, so I was spared finding myself tagged the next morning.

The party was well underway by the time I arrived. My disguise was surprisingly effective. Nobody knew who I was until I sashayed over to Bob Alfandre who recognized me when I spoke to him and he roared with laughter. He dragged me around the party introducing me left and right saying, "Meet my priest! This is my priest!" Connie was a big hit. In the middle of much darkness, we shared a light and cheerful moment.

Two weeks later on a Sunday evening, ten of us gathered in Ron's room to celebrate his sixth anniversary of sobriety in AA. My diary from that day states, "Spent whole evening with Ron at hospital. It was wonderful." Ron led the meeting, and he chose the theme of gratitude. We were in a state of grace. We had been told by the hospital staff that Ron would be discharged the following Saturday, and I couldn't wait to have him all to myself again.

Dr. Bruni, Ron's regular doctor, had treated Ron for several years, and they adored each other, but Dr. Bruni was out of town. When I visited the hospital the day after our AA meeting in Ron's hospital room, I met with a different doctor. He said to me point blank, "Well, you know he's dying." Well, no, I did not. I'd spent many hours over the years talking with families whose loved ones were dying, and I'd had many difficult conversations about whether to terminate treatment when further medical intervention seemed futile. Yet, I had not had that conversation with myself, nor with Ron or the medical staff. I was in denial. Losing Ron was a thought I'd never fully admitted to consciousness.

On Wednesday of that week, I went to see Ron in the late afternoon, and we spent a couple of hours together. He was in a good mood. His parents had brought in his chihuahua, Big Red, when they'd visited that afternoon, and that had cheered him up no end. He'd also tried to walk that day for the first time in a long while. I lay down beside him on the bed. He was warmly playful and affectionate. He took a call from Bob Gray, and they spoke at great length about going to Hawaii together again. Before I left, I told Ron, "I may not be able to come to the hospital tomorrow. I have a hectic day, and there's a special service at the cathedral where we're officially installing Bishop Haines as the head bishop." I explained that Bishop Haines had asked me personally to participate, and I told Ron I'd try to come by to see him if I could. "Besides," I added, "you're coming home on Saturday!"

I turned to him as I left the room and lingered in the doorway. We locked eyes for a long time. This is something I normally wouldn't do, but that night we'd connected even more deeply than usual. I didn't want to leave.

I'd left Ron at around seven o'clock to attend yet another seemingly endless ECRA committee meeting. After the meeting, I stopped by Steve Lembesis' house to return the drag outfit he'd loaned me for the Halloween party. Steve had been a fantastic ECRA board president, and I'd often thanked God for his being there. He was a flaming liberal from Alabama, a charming and highly intelligent man. Steve and his lover had started the "Miss Adams Morgan Pageant" in his living room, a drag event that soon became an enormous ballroom fundraiser and continues to this day. Steve and I got caught up watching a videotape of the latest fundraising pageant, and that's what I was doing when Ron died at 10:30 that evening, Wednesday, November 14, 1990.

I got the call at 11p.m. letting me know that the love of my life was gone. I drove directly to the hospital. A nurse was waiting for me in the dimly lit lobby. She took me straight to Ron's room and left us alone. I've often wished I'd known her name because of her gentle acts of kindness. She'd waited for me, so I wouldn't have to walk through the darkened hospital corridors alone that night, and she'd arranged for me to have time alone with Ron on the night he died.

That last visit with Ron was extraordinary. We shared a sacred space. I talked to him. I stroked his face and quietly sang Amazing Grace. I was amazed that he looked so much like his old self. I may have been hallucinating, but he looked radiant. I recalled the theme of our last AA meeting and felt a profound sense of gratitude just to be with him as I said goodbye.

An hour and a half later, Ron's sister Marsha and her husband, Andy, arrived. Thankfully, Ron's parents didn't come because they tended to get hysterical at such moments. It was lovely to see Marsha and Andy, and their timing was just right. I'd had my time alone with Ron, and now it was time for his favorite sister to say her farewell.

Before I left that night, the hospital staff told me that Ron had gone into cardiac arrest, and they'd performed CPR on him for quite some time. I was shocked to hear that, because it made me realize how utterly unprepared we'd been for the worst. We had never even discussed "do not resuscitate" orders, or anything else of that nature. I looked at my diary entry for the upcoming Saturday and saw through my tears the words, "Ron comes home from the hospital. Hallelujah!"
I drove home and tried to sleep.

The next morning was spent making phone calls to family and friends. I cancelled a few appointments, but I made it to the cathedral for Bishop Haines' installation. I was a walking zombie. I went through the motions of administering communion, then I went home and drew a bath. I'm not one for taking baths, but I was all alone and yearned to feel an enveloping warmth. The apartment had been extremely quiet for weeks without Ron's enlivening presence. Just as I slid down into the warm bath water, Ron's hairbrush fell with a loud bang from the shelf on the opposite wall of the bathroom. It made me smile.

Lida and Robert held a funeral mass for Ron at their Catholic church out in Virginia, where they had been praying for Ron's healing from "cancer" for the past year or so. They didn't want people to know their son had AIDS. Since they hadn't come to hospital to see Ron right after he died, we went out to the morgue together, so they could view his body.

Morgues are depressing. Ron's body was stone cold on a gurney under a sheet, but the Bushnells had to pose and take pictures with him. I refused to have my picture taken with Ron dead. He was going to be cremated, so perhaps that accounted for their decision. Of course, they had a right to grieve in whatever way they found appropriate.

The Roman Catholic priest invited me to participate in the funeral mass Ron's parents had arranged at their church in Mt. Vernon. He asked me to read from the Gospel and to stand next to him at the altar when he blessed the bread and wine. As we lined up for the procession, however, he turned to me and said, "But you can't receive communion." Roman Catholics have a lot of rules about who can receive communion, and rule number one is that you have to be Roman Catholic. I thought to myself, "So I can make Jesus with you, but I can't eat Jesus with you." I laughed on the inside. I'd been concelebrating and receiving with Catholic priests for years at our AIDS retreats, but that was not to be in this church.

I spent Thanksgiving Day at Marsha and Andy's house, along with their daughters Lisa and Julia, and it was a tender and healing time for me. Late that afternoon, I went down to their den and took a nap. When I awoke from my nap, I looked out through the sliding glass doors at a pink and purple sky, the colors of the flowers we'd chosen for our own memorial service for Ron. In the back yard I saw a cardinal perched on the branch of a nearby tree and four doves on a wire. I felt Ron's presence deeply at that moment and have always thought of him when I've seen cardinals in the years since.

It was months before I was fully grounded in myself again. I was lingering between two worlds: the world of the physical and the world of the spirit.

While my nephew Darrin was living with us the August before Ron died, he came home one afternoon to find Ron working happily away on his own plans for his funeral. Darrin told me Ron was in his usual upbeat, expansive mood. The windows were open to let in the summer breeze, and Dead Can Dance was singing Toward the Within on the CD player. Ron had discussed his funeral at some length with a few people, so we had a good starting point as we began making plans.

Ron wanted a string quartet to play Samuel Barber's Adagio for Strings, so I knew it was going to be a big affair and cost a lot of money. The other thing I knew for sure was that it was going to be exactly the way Ron wanted it.

I called the Bushnells from Marsha's place and asked to come over and talk with them about the funeral arrangements. I needed financial help for this big event. Knowing this could become a difficult conversation, Marsha asked to accompany me, so we drove over to the Bushnell residence together. We sat down with Ron's parents and one of his other sisters in the living room. Lida and I went over my preliminary plans, and then I came to the hard part—asking for money. The service and trip to Hawaii to scatter his ashes were going to cost around $3,000, so I asked, "Can you give me $1,000 toward the funeral?"

At that point, Ron's father broke in with, "I haven't even seen any details!" When I handed him Ron's written instructions, he looked them over and rasped, "Well, this looks like a big show to me." I took a deep breath and said, "Mr. Bushnell, you don't have to come to the funeral if you don't want to." I'd just about had enough of dealing with his belligerent, abusive personality. That's all it took to send him into a rage. Marsha got between the two of us and played the role she'd always played of defending Ron's best interests against their hard-nosed, homophobic father.

Lida quickly wrote me a check for $1,000, and I rushed out of their house. I needn't have worried. Lida, with her outsized personality, wanted a big funeral even more than Ron or I did. She expanded on Ron's already ambitious ideas considerably, so it was grander than even he had imagined. She turned it into the equivalent of a Royal Samoan state funeral.

CHAPTER THIRTY-SIX

Ron's Funeral and Afterwards

Lida could be a delightfully charming human being. She could also be difficult and controlling. In this case, both aspects of her personality helped bring off a celebration of Ron's life that would have thrilled him to the core.

Lida wanted the funeral to reflect Ron's royal Samoan heritage, and so it did. The funeral was held December 1st in St. Patrick's church where Ron had been received into the Episcopal Church only months before. The Samoan community attended the service in traditional Samoan dress with leis. The Samoan flag was prominently displayed, and the Samoan Delegate to the U.S. House of Representatives was dressed in a native skirt as he addressed the congregation. The Samoans sang a beautiful Samoan hymn that was particularly moving. Laid out in front of the urn holding Ron's ashes was a beautifully decorated fabric that the King of Tonga—Lida's cousin—had previously sent for Ron's grandmother's funeral.

My friend Marge Nichols adored Ron and had flown in from Dallas for the funeral. We were seated together with my sister Thelma and nephew Darrin who'd come from Herrin. Seated next to us were the Bushnells, complete with their grumpy patriarch. As Ron would have wanted it, the four speakers who took the podium generated a great deal of humor, and the room was alive with laughter. Some of the tales they told were bawdy as well as funny. Ron's father, however, maintained his grim demeanor the entire time. I wanted to lean over and say to him, "You son of a bitch, you never did give your son a chance, and you're not going to do it even now."

The four speakers, of whom I was one, included Bob Gray whose partner, Bill Austin, had died a month earlier; Ron's sister, Marsha; and Ben Usher, a retired federal judge and friend of Ron's from AA. I told stories that highlighted Ron's generosity to strangers and how he'd taught me to be more accepting of the poor, the homeless, and the downtrodden. Ron always gave money to the homeless, even though he had little to give. I also talked about what Ron had meant to me. I'd been blessed by many angels in earthly form over the course of my life and ministry, and Ron was chief among them. He was my archangel, and I feel embraced by his guardian love to this day.

I'd bought 500 carnations for the ushers to hand out to everyone who came to the funeral, and that wasn't enough. Close to 700 people attended Ron's funeral. I was overwhelmed by the turnout. It was a deeply moving and spiritually powerful occasion. Diane Rehm attended and talked about the experience on her radio show the next day.

Ron's instructions were that I should take his ashes to Kona on the Big Island of Hawaii and scatter them there. Ron had visited Kona several times with Bob Gray and Bill Austin, and he loved it. He'd told me about his favorite spot on the western side of the island where he'd watch the whales mate in the deep water just off the coast in wintertime—except he didn't use the word "mate." That's where Ron wanted me to scatter his ashes.

Ron did not want his parents to have control of his ashes, and Marsha had warned me that if they ever got their hands on them, I'd never get them back. At the end of the service, when everyone's emotions were running deep, Lida asked me if she could keep her son's ashes at home until I took them to Hawaii. It was difficult to deny her request, so I agreed with some trepidation.

After the reception that followed the funeral, we invited AA members in attendance to join us downstairs for an AA meeting. About 150 of us gathered together and told more stories and shared more laughter. We wrapped things up around 7 p.m. and walked outside to find a magnificent full moon high in the sky overhead. "Of course, Ron would arrange for a full moon to honor the goddess," someone said with a smile. Ron had always been adept at finding ways to honor the goddess of nature.

After it was all over, I was deeply grateful that we'd honored

Ron so lovingly and so well. Even though it differed a little from his own plans, he would have loved every moment.

The holidays were difficult, and it would take time before life returned to normal. On December 23, my former partner Terry and his current partner, Chuck, invited me to a Christmas party at their townhouse. Terry's parents were there along with a lot of other people I knew, and they were all happy to see me. The party wasn't all that different from those Terry and I had hosted together three years before, and it brought back poignant memories.

I left early to have dinner with Ron's sister and her family. As I stepped through the door into the cold night air, I paused for a moment to reflect on everything that had happened. I realized that the game had been worth the candle. Even if I'd known from the beginning that I'd lose Ron as I had, I would have done it all over again. Our time together was worth the present sorrow. I walked on out under the stars with no regrets.

On Christmas Eve, I had dinner with Matt McGarvey and Victor Indrosandro. Victor was still in a wheelchair due to his neuropathy, and Matt now had to carry him up and down the steps of their townhouse. We had a lovely time together, and then I left to attend Midnight Mass at St. Patrick's. On Christmas Day, I flew home to Herrin and my family. It was time to go back to the land where my ancestors had settled before the Civil War. I needed to return to my roots. After arriving in Herrin, I hit the road and spent the next ten days driving all over Illinois visiting relatives and friends.

My first stop was Champaign, where I visited my friend Ed Winslow who was HIV-positive and would be dead from AIDS within four years. I then drove on to Chicago where I'd been ordained and lived for eight years.

I visited various friends in the Chicago area and had an early New Year's Eve dinner with Ray and Jean Britt whom I knew from my days at St. Augustine's parish in Wilmette. This was the first time I had seen them since getting sober. At midnight, following an AA meeting, I found myself standing on the shore of Lake Michigan looking up at a full moon. We'd had a full moon on December 1st for Ron's memorial service, and now there was a second one to welcome the New Year. It was a moment when Ron would have "blessed the goddess." It was another perfect moment, and I realized I was no longer grief-stricken but at peace. I felt deep humility and gratitude for the gift of having loved and been loved by so many people, both living and dead.

While in Illinois, I learned that Bill Barcus, one of my personal heroes who had electrified us all as the keynote speaker of our first AIDS conference, had flown home to Wichita, Kansas to die. I wanted to see him while it was still possible, so I called to ask if I could drive out for a brief visit. "Don't come," he said. "I'm terribly sick, and there's been a blizzard out here. Everybody's stranded." Bill died a month later.

Soon after my conversation with Bill, a former classmate from seminary invited me to go skiing with him in Iowa. We skied on the bluffs overlooking Mississippi River—yes, it's possible to ski in Iowa. My winter getaway was helping enormously. I could feel myself growing ever more centered.

Before returning to Washington, I drove to Springfield to spend a few days with my Aunt Tootsie who was my mother's youngest sister. While there, I visited the tomb of Abraham Lincoln, a man I'd admired my entire life. I visited the cemetery on a crystal-clear Friday morning. The sky was blue, and snow crunched under my feet. There had always been a large crowd of visitors when I'd visited before, but that morning I was the only person paying my respects at Lincoln's final resting place. Since I had the place to myself, I quietly sang Amazing Grace, just as I had sung it for Ron on the night he died. It was the perfect place for me to connect with Ron, alone with the Lincolns who had also suffered great loss. Once again, I'd been granted a perfect moment of love, of healing, and of rest.

CHAPTER THIRTY-SEVEN

BARBARA MCCONAGHA

The plague years were full of sad stories, but there was no shortage of humor, especially gallows humor, throughout the epidemic. One of the funniest people I've ever met is a Washington playwright named Barbara McConagha. I met her soon after starting my AIDS ministry. Even though she was Jewish, she was a founding member of Damien Ministries, the Catholic AIDS organization.

Barbara attended our first interfaith retreat at the Catholic retreat center in West Virginia. She had never been on a Christian retreat before and wasn't sure how to dress. She settled on a stylish black leather pant suit. The gay guys just assumed she was a lesbian.

Barbara had gone to a private girls school in her youth, and a majority of the students, who were Episcopalians, treated her as an outsider. They knew the rules but wouldn't tell her what they were. Barbara has taken her revenge over the years by making jokes about Episcopalians at every opportunity. Every play she has written at least one joke at our expense. I consider her a cross between Joan Rivers and Erma Bombeck.

A couple of my AIDS ministry board members were so offended by her jokes that they demanded I have nothing more to do with her. There was no way that was going to happen. I needed all the laughter I could get.

Barbara became quite successful as a playwright later on, but I remember a remarkable preview reading of a work-in-progress from her earlier years that was less than a triumph. It was a draft play about a woman who'd been born as a pig. Curious how a feminist playwright would handle such a premise, I took a friend, Sheldon Golum, who was also Jewish to see the preview with me. Sheldon had AIDS and had become an accomplished inspirational speaker. He'd been a great comfort to my friend Logan, and I admired him as he encouraged others while courageously fighting his own battle.

The night of the reading, Sheldon and I were seated in the theater several rows back from Barbara and her husband and two sons. The audience had trouble grasping what the play was all about. Midway through the reading, I noticed that Barbara had left her seat. I found her during the intermission with her head in her hands in the back of the theater. She knew then that the play would bomb and never completed it.

Sheldon died a week later. Barbara always said she was convinced it was her play that killed him!

CHAPTER THIRTY-EIGHT

LIFE GOES ON

My Illinois trip was every bit as grounding and restorative as I'd hoped it would be. I returned to Washington eager to attend Melody Gilsey's second big AIDS gala on February 8, 1991. It was almost two years since the last one. Once again, Barbara Bush agreed to be honorary chair of the gala committee. It was scheduled for just before Mardi Gras, so the theme was Carnival! Melody hired Brazilian samba dancers with glorious, over-the-top costumes and brilliantly feathered headdresses. The skimpily clad muscular men were practically naked, so the atmosphere was both colorful and sensuous.

The dancing began on the stage, and then the performers came down on the floor to dance for the individual tables. I had positioned myself in the back of the room. It had been a little over two months since Ron's death, and I wasn't yet in a dancing spirit. I was pleased the event was happening, but I wasn't fully engaged. We had convinced Bishop Haines to come, and he seemed to be having a good time. His eyes sparkled when a beautiful black female dancer had a "wardrobe malfunction" right in front of him, and one of her breasts fell out of her costume. Melody Gilsey didn't miss a beat. She jumped up, grabbed the hand of her husband, Peter, and signaled to everyone present that it was time to start dancing. Everybody flowed out on the dance floor, and the lovely Brazilian dancer melted into the crowd. Melody had turned an awkward moment into party time.

The timing for the gala was fortunate because President Bush would soon order the invasion of Kuwait. Funding for AIDS soon declined as war tightened the purse strings.

The church was changing. On the day after Ron died, Bishop Haines was installed as the new bishop of the Diocese of Washington. He'd been acting in that capacity for months following the death of the late Bishop Walker prior to his election. We'd been in seminary together, and I found it much easier to work with him. He was openly supportive of our AIDS ministry and didn't criticize my involvement in the gay community. My erstwhile nemesis, Provost Charles Perry, was gone and his replacement, Sanford Garner, was the former rector of Christ Church in Georgetown who'd helped raise funds for an AIDS ministry early in the epidemic. These were positive developments at a time when we especially needed them. Many of the people who'd attended our retreats and healing services were beginning to die, and I was spending much more time at funerals and memorial services.

CHAPTER THIRTY-NINE

ASHES

Before I could plan my trip to Hawaii to scatter Ron's ashes, I had to figure out how to get them back from Lida without causing an uproar. I talked to Marsha about it, and she hit on the perfect solution: "Why don't you ask Bishop Montgomery to come to their house, and we'll tell my parents that you're bringing the bishop to say prayers with them as they separate from Ron's ashes." Ron's parents would probably go along with this because they were big on religious ceremony. Lida didn't know it, but Bishop Montgomery, who'd ordained me all those years ago in Chicago, was now living in Northern Virginia and had a very loving pastoral touch.

Our scheme worked. Bishop Montgomery couldn't have been more gracious when we visited Ron's parents on a Sunday afternoon. Overwhelmed by the bishop's presence, Lida and Robert handed over Ron's ashes without a murmur. This time, I didn't have to charge out of the house in a fury. Mercifully, I was able to fulfill Ron's last wish without fighting his parents.

On March 21, I flew to Herrin to celebrate my parents' 68th wedding anniversary and my 49th birthday. I'm glad I made the trip that year, because it was the last time I ever saw my mother.

Following our celebrations, I flew on to Hawaii with Ron's ashes and joined two close friends, Alex McGehee and Donald AuCoin, in Kona. It was comforting to have them there as I carried out Ron's last wishes. We scattered Ron's ashes into the Pacific Ocean on Good Friday at sunset. As we turned back toward the mountains, we were once again graced by the rising full moon, the Easter Moon.

When I left the Big Island, I flew to the island of Molokai

where Father Damien, a Belgian Roman Catholic monk, had cared for the physical and spiritual needs of lepers living under quarantine in the latter quarter of the 19th century. Father Damien had volunteered to serve the leper colony as a priest and asked to stay on beyond his assigned term. He ultimately caught leprosy and died at the colony at the age of 49.

I had long wanted to visit Father Damien's Molokai shrine and to see the place where he'd served out his ministry and the last years of his life. Having just celebrated my own 49th birthday, I felt this was a propitious time to be making my pilgrimage. The former leper colony was naturally isolated at the foot of high cliffs where about four acres formed a small peninsula pushing out into the sea. Life wasn't easy for people with leprosy. Sometimes they were taken out to the colony by boat and made to swim ashore. The only way I could get there was by riding a mule with a group of other pilgrims down a steep, circuitous path leading to the base of the cliffs.

Father Damien was made a saint by the Roman Catholic Church in 2009, but many of us considered him the patron saint of AIDS patients long before that. I was inspired by his example in my own ministry. Ignorant people who didn't know any better viewed both leprosy and AIDS as punishment by God for sexual sins. Father Damien himself was falsely accused of sexual impropriety when he contracted leprosy. He is honored today not only by the Roman Catholic Church but also by the Episcopal Church which celebrates his feast day on April 15.

Damien was a carpenter and built the chapel that still stands on the grounds of his beloved leper colony. I prayed in that chapel, giving thanks for my life and work and asking for God's continuing guidance and mercy in the years ahead. I carry within an enduring connection to the sacred spaces where I scattered Ron's ashes and visited Fr. Damien's shrine.

CHAPTER FORTY

LOVE COMES CALLING AGAIN

I returned from Hawaii just in time to go on another AIDS retreat in April. The theme of this retreat was "Grief and Loss." By now, everybody attending the retreat had lost someone close, often more than one. On the first day of the retreat, I sat out on the hillside taking in the view. It was a lovely spring afternoon, and many of the retreatants were out for a walk.

That's how I met Doug. I first saw him as he walked down the hill from where I was sitting. He was wearing short shorts, had muscular legs, and was blonde and cute. I later learned that he loved to run marathons. Doug was HIV-positive and had come on this retreat because he was grieving the loss of his AIDS buddy, who'd recently died.

Doug and I took a liking to each other, and I was surprised and unsettled to find myself interested in someone else so soon after losing Ron. We began dating after the retreat, but I was afraid to tell anyone. I was still in mourning for Ron, and I felt I was betraying him. It seemed too soon; only five months had passed.

On Mother's Day, I visited a friend, Mitch, in New York who was dying of AIDS and had recently been hospitalized. Ron and I had stayed with Mitch and his lover, Deepak, on our last trip to Manhattan. I called my mother from their apartment to wish her a happy Mother's Day. She had adored Ron, and she brought him up in conversation. She said, "You know, it wasn't that we didn't like Terry, but there was something special about Ron." She couldn't believe he was dead. Then, in one of mom's classic maneuvers to see past the veil of my privacy, she asked, "Are you seeing anyone else?" "No," I said, "I'm not ready." That was the last conversation I had with my mother before she died, and I told her a white lie. I think about that every Mother's Day.

Doug and I grew closer as the year rolled on. We began camping together, one of Doug's favorite activities. We'd head out to West Virginia doing the typical camping thing, and I soon grew to love it, too. It was a much-needed escape from what had become a seemingly endless stream of AIDS deaths. It reminded me that I was alive.

On the morning of June 13, my father awoke to find my mother unresponsive and called an ambulance. She'd had a massive stroke at the age of 86. I was scheduled to attend the ordination of my good friend Jean Rogers at the National Cathedral two days later so decided not to rush home to Herrin since my mother was unconscious. Late the following evening as I was praying for my mother and for Ron, my sister called to tell me that our mother had died at 10:30. She died seven months to the day, and at the same hour, as Ron. I like to think he was waiting for her on the other side.

It was a warm summer's evening, so I went to sleep with the windows wide open. About three o'clock in the morning, I was awakened by a fox howling loudly outside my window. I got out of bed, looked out toward the woods, and saw him sitting right there in the middle of the yard. "My God, it's a fox!" I exclaimed. With that, the fox ran off into the woods. I'm convinced my mother was playing with me. I could almost hear her saying, "Well, you didn't come to me, so I came to you!"

I flew home immediately after Jean's ordination service and officiated at my mother's funeral along with two Pentecostal ministers. Grief-stricken by her loss, my father pined away before dying just a few years later at the age of 92. I conducted his funeral with the same two ministers in 1994.

I continued to date Doug into the summer, and word of our relationship was getting around. Jack Harris and others questioned my sanity. I'd been immersed in the epidemic for so long that they probably thought I should give myself a break. Jim

Graham, an AIDS advocate and director of the Whitman-Walker Clinic, asked me to dinner one night. "How do you do it?" he asked. He wanted to know how I could do AIDS ministry all day with people who were dying and then come home to somebody with AIDS. I had no good answer for him. These were the people I was surrounded by. These were the people in my life. Life was intense, and it was short.

Early on, as Doug and I were riding our bikes together, I noticed he had a pack of cigarettes in his fanny pack, and I had a panic attack on the spot. All I saw was death. Losing friends to death was taking its toll on me. I couldn't help comparing Doug to Ron, who'd been such a health nut. That was unfair to Doug, of course. One of the things that appealed to me about Doug, however, was that he, like Ron and me, was an AIDS warrior. He was out there helping people. Plus, he was in AA, and he was fun to be with.

Doug worked as the night manager at an exclusive restaurant in Amtrak's Union Station complex not far from the U.S. Capitol. It was a magnificent space, and high-level dignitaries often dined there. One night that summer when Congress wasn't in session and business was slow, Doug invited me to join him at the restaurant. When I arrived, he'd dimmed the lights, and candles decorated the tables. We sat down to a delicious salmon dinner as lovely music played in the background, and then we danced. It was a memorably romantic evening.

Not long after that, Doug was interviewed by NBC Evening News for a story on a new experimental drug to treat AIDS. Up until then, the only drug approved for that purpose had been AZT, but it didn't seem to be doing anybody much good and carried severe side effects. When a second drug, DDI, was approved, Doug signed on to try it. When he heard that NBC was doing a story on DDI and asking to talk with people who were taking it, he agreed to be on the show.

After the interview, Doug called to tell me what he'd done and said, "I doubt anyone at the restaurant would have seen it, because they're all too busy working." I thought to myself, "Oh my God, the whole world watches NBC News," but I didn't say anything. We learned the next day that even his cousins in Canada had seen the interview, and within a week Doug was fired from his job.

Naturally, he was deeply upset at the loss of his job and his income. To help with expenses while he looked for another job, I suggested he move in with me, and he did. In hindsight, that might have been a mistake. The apartment was still something of a shrine to Ron, but sometimes one has to learn things the hard way. In any case, my offer was well-intentioned. I had extra space, and Doug was struggling. We had fun together, and we shared a common cause as fellow crusaders in the war against AIDS.

Later in 1991, I signed up to be a guinea pig for the new AIDS vaccine trials taking place at Johns Hopkins Hospital in Baltimore, 45 miles from Washington. For almost two years, I drove to Baltimore every month to have my blood drawn. I needed to be pro-active in finding a cure for AIDS and wanted to do whatever I could to help push things along. The alternative was feeling help-less. In trials like these, some people are given a placebo, but after it was over, I found out I actually did get the trial vaccine.

That August, the Episcopal Church held its triennial General Convention in Phoenix, Arizona. By now we were pretty much all on the same page in acknowledging the AIDS epidemic. The Church was beginning to recognize the dignity and worth of gay men and women, and the Convention passed resolutions encouraging each diocese to establish a dialogue between its gay and straight communities. Washington's Bishop Haines had ordained an avowed lesbian to the priesthood in June. After the Convention, he encouraged gay men and lesbians to share their experiences with local parishes. Doug and I volunteered through-out 1991 and 1992 to visit various parishes, talk about our lives, and answer questions. For the most part, people treated us kindly.

With Doug's assistance, I continued the weekly AIDS healing service Ron and I had started at St. Thomas' Church in Dupont Circle. Later, we added evening services at All Souls Church with a dinner afterwards. As a way of getting other parishes involved, we'd invite a different parish to cook dinner for each service, and they were marvelous in their support. When the ECRA ministry started in 1987, we'd had the support of only sixteen Episcopal parishes. By 1996, thirty-seven parishes were participating.

CHAPTER FORTY-ONE

MILITARY FUNERALS

In the 1990s, the question of accepting gays in the military was a hot political issue. I had the privilege of officiating at the funerals of four gay soldiers at Arlington National Cemetery. Bill Clinton had become president in 1993 pledging to end the ban on gays in the military. Opposition by military and congressional leaders ultimately led to a notorious compromise, the so-called "don't ask, don't tell" policy. This policy prohibited discrimination against closeted homosexual service members while banning people who were openly gay from serving. Thousands of gay and lesbian military members had already been dishonorably discharged. It did offer some protection to gay men and women already serving who were willing to hide their homosexuality to save their careers.

Clinton openly supported the AIDS community. Doug and I marched in his inauguration parade with the People with AIDS Coalition. We marched with the mother of Ryan White, a teenage hemophiliac infected during a blood transfusion who was kicked out of school for being HIV-positive.

Two of the military funerals I conducted for gay men were especially memorable for the full military honors that accompanied them. In 1989, a popular doctor who had previously served as an officer in the Army died of AIDS. His partner called and asked me to do the funeral at Arlington Cemetery. He told me it would be done with full honors. In this case, that meant a military band, a riderless horse, use of the caisson to carry the coffin, an Honor Guard of six soldiers bearing flags, and a rifle salute at the graveside.

Prior to the funeral, the deceased doctor's lover and I visited

Fort Myer, the Army base next to Arlington Cemetery, to organize the service with two mid-rank officers. I'd done a couple of military funerals by now, so I knew the routine. This visit, however, was awkward. The officers were as nervous as I was, and they were trying to be polite and businesslike. When I needed to use the men's room, one officer said he'd escort me. When we arrived at the men's room, he didn't wait outside the door; he followed me right into the men's room and used the urinal next to me while keeping intense eye contact with me the whole time. It was most unsettling.

There was a large turnout for the funeral. At least 200 people showed up, and about three-quarters of them were gay men in stylish suits and ties. The military allows only half an hour for the chapel service at Arlington, so the schedule runs fairly tight. The soloist delayed our start by getting into an argument with the organist just before the service began. The decedent's grieving partner was a bit on the emotional side and took a little extra time to get settled. We ran over by five minutes, a violation that would come back to haunt me later.

A Baptist military chaplain was provided to escort us from the chapel to the burial site. He was uncommonly chatty, making breezy remarks as we walked along behind the Honor Guard.

"How did the good doctor get infected, anyway?" he asked. Under the circumstances, this struck me as odd, to say the least. "I've no idea," I replied curtly. "I wasn't there, and I haven't seen a videotape."

The chaplain then expounded on the way in which the soldiers in the Honor Guard walking ahead of us "like to play with each other with their shoulders—they lean in kind of hard." He seemed to be suggesting that the Honor Guard were getting cozy with each other on the formal, ten minute procession to the graveside. It was a thoroughly bizarre conversation.

Once my mind was launched in that direction, it kept up under its own steam. I was in a military environment that sought to keep homosexuality in the dark. It fostered repression at a time when many gay people wanted to step out into the light and lead authentic lives. The setting beckoned my mind to dark places. Next to the cemetery were the grounds of the Iwo Jima Marine Memorial that had once been a gay cruising area. About the time I moved to Washington, a young congressional staffer had been beaten there and left to die. That area had a long history of illicit sex and murder until the brush was cleared away.

My final dark thought before coming back to reality arose as the Honor Guard fired its salute. I imagined an outbreak of internalized homophobia causing them to fire their guns on me and the gay mourners.

The other military funeral that stands out from those years took place in 1994. Terry, my former partner, called me on a Sunday afternoon and asked me to come to the emergency room. His lover, Chuck Magness, had had a bad accident. He'd been up on the roof of their townhouse cleaning the windows that morning when he slipped and fell, hitting his head on a brick wall below. He didn't survive the fall.

Chuck was a fine man, and I liked him a lot. He'd served as a military officer and had worked hard after his retirement to overturn the ban on gays in the military. He was also HIV-positive and an active crusader on that front. The Washington Post had run a front-page feature story about his efforts, photo and all. When Terry asked me to officiate at the funeral, I learned that it, too, would include full military honors.

Although Chuck had come out as gay and had been living with Terry for some time, he was married during his time in the military. He and his wife had never actually divorced, so there was a question as to who would get the flag at the graveside once it was folded: Chuck's wife or the gay partner with whom he had shared his life for several years. The young undertaker, fresh out of mortuary school, nervously suggested that two flags be placed over the coffin, one for each. "Who," I thought to myself, "is going to call the officers at Fort Myer and make that request?!"

We all breathed a collective sigh of relief when Chuck's wife came up with a thoughtful solution that worked for everyone. Terry and Chuck's wife would sit together, and when the flag was given to her, she would pass it on to him.

A different chaplain was assigned to me on this occasion. He took me aside and sternly inquired how long the service would take. "The last time you had one of these AIDS funerals," he said, "you went five minutes over." I was surprised that they not only remembered me from five years earlier but seemed still offended that we hadn't stuck within the strict thirty minute time limit. "No more than thirty minutes, sir!" I replied.

CHAPTER FORTY-TWO

SOUTH AFRICA

Desmond Tutu, the world-renowned Anglican Archbishop of Cape Town, South Africa, had been a good friend of Bishop Walker and visited Washington frequently. He was an early supporter of gay rights in his own country. In 1994, a South African man named Gary Lamont was fired from his staff position in a Cape Town church when he attempted to secure support for AIDS relief and came out as gay. Bishop Tutu got involved and supported Gary in starting the first faith-based AIDS organization in Cape Town and allowed it to operate out of St. George's Cathedral. Gary had heard of our AIDS ministry in Washington and visited us to see how we operated. Our two organizations began to share information and ideas. He invited us to send two members of our flock to participate in Cape Town's World AIDS Day activities in December of 1994.

We sent Nalty Keleen and Maxwell Lawton. Nalty was a stand-up comic and drag queen from New Orleans who told timeless stories about growing up in a traditionally Roman Catholic family. He loved his blind grandmother but couldn't tell her that he, too, was losing his eyesight due to AIDS. She wasn't supposed to know he was sick.

Max was also from an old southern family, but his relatives were Baptist preachers and missionaries. I'd visited him several times in the hospital when he was admitted with AIDS-related infections. Max was a graduate student at Wesley Theological Seminary in D.C where he was studying theology and art. He painted works of art that frequently disturbed excessively pious Christians. Nalty and Max were great guys, and both were struggling with their health.

When they got to Cape Town, they dived right in to help Gary and his organization with their contributions to World AIDS Day. Nalty did seven stand-up performances in drag and became something of a star. Maxwell became Artist-in-Residence at St. George's Cathedral where his controversial painting of a naked Jesus with AIDS stirred up an angry response. The painting portrayed Jesus with Kaposi's sarcoma lesions, an IV drip, and an oxygen tube. Predictably, some found the painting blasphemous and heretical. Threats were made against both Maxwell and the painting, which prompted the bishop to defend it publicly. It made news across the world.

Although Maxwell's painting ultimately eclipsed Nalty's work in notoriety, I delighted in telling people that our ministry was the first to send a missionary to South Africa in drag. The Washington Post published a long article with pictures about our representatives to Cape Town. Bishop Haines never said a word of reproof.

Nalty died a month after he returned home. Maxwell survived AIDS and lived on until 2006.

Shortly after Nalty and Maxwell returned from the World AIDS Day celebrations, I visited Gary Lamont in South Africa for two weeks. We conducted a healing service together and visited a squatters' shantytown where Gary had established a cottage crafts center to earn money for women with AIDS. He introduced me to the mind-boggling extent of suffering caused by AIDS in his country. The scale of poverty and inequality in South Africa was enormous. The Truth and Reconciliation Commission to understand and heal human rights violations that had taken place under apartheid had just assembled. I heard a priest preach a sermon at St. George's Cathedral supporting the healing process. He'd lost both his hands to a letter bomb as a result of his opposition to apartheid. His sermon was deeply inspiring in his call for forgiveness.

We drove north to the Indian Ocean, where I took a swim, and then further north to visit a game preserve. We camped near a watering hole and waited until the predawn hours to see a myriad of creatures emerge until the heat of the day drove them back. After that, we drove through Zululand. All in all, it was an exotic experience for a boy from Herrin, Illinois. At the end of my stay, I flew home from Johannesburg feeling rested and restored.

Just two years later, President Nelson Mandela promulgated South Africa's post-apartheid constitution. It was the first in the world to ban discrimination based on sexual orientation.

Doug picked me up at the airport and drove us home. Just as we were settling down in the living room, he turned to me and said, "I was in the hospital last week. They diagnosed me with pneumocystis pneumonia." I burst into tears. I couldn't believe it. I put my head in his lap and cried like a baby. "I didn't want to ruin your trip," he told me, "so I didn't call you with the news."

South Africa had been a welcome reprieve, but now the battle was to be joined again, this time with Doug. Now that he'd been diagnosed with full-blown AIDS, Doug quit his job and went on disability.

This was a crisis for Doug's family as well. They knew he was gay and had come to terms with it as best they could. When he'd come out as a teenager, they spent thousands of dollars on a psychiatrist who hospitalized him for a month in an effort to make him straight. Doug ran away from home and was out of touch with his family for some time. They did come around eventually. They'd learned he'd been diagnosed as HIV-positive when he was 25; he was now 38 years old.

That summer his parents, seven of his eight siblings, and many nieces and nephews rented two large houses on the Outer Banks of North Carolina for a week. The family had not been together for a long time. It was as if they thought he was going to die. I tried to relax and have a good time, but Doug was running fevers and sneaking around smoking cigarettes. One evening I asked him if he would walk down to the water with me. We sat on the bench for a while. I felt so weary and laid my head in his lap. That's when a horrible thought came to my mind and I realized I had to say it out loud. I quietly said, "Why don't I get a gun and shoot you and then kill myself." Needless to say, I did not do that. During this time Doug was on disability and continued to struggle to stay as well as he could.

CHAPTER FORTY-THREE

High Noon at ECRA

The board for the Episcopal Caring Response to AIDS had become increasingly unwieldy. By mid-1994, we had seventy-four members on the board, and twenty of them served on the executive committee, which met monthly. There was no executive director. It was a board-run volunteer operation and really needed a strong director at the helm to stay focused. Steve Lembesis, the much beloved chair of the board, had died of AIDS one year before. He'd done an excellent job of herding cats and keeping the excessively large board focused on essentials, but now he was gone. Steve's death was a deep personal loss. I had loved and depended on him. Without his firm guidance, the organization had gradually become an ungovernable mess.

Matters came to a head that summer. The work of the organization was challenging and intense, and I was burning out. It didn't help when the board fired our office manager, Billy. ECRA had only two paid staff members: yours truly and Billy. Billy had been a key player in the organization from the beginning, but his partner had died the year before, and he'd become unmoored. The board's firing of Billy created substantial discord, and we all felt the absence of Steve Lembesis' astute leadership.

Disagreement over who would replace Billy proved even more contentious than the decision to fire him. By the summer of 1995, I'd had enough and announced I would resign at the end of the year. I'd soon wish I'd made it easier on myself and the organization by leaving immediately.

Several board members began painting me as a villain and the cause of all the organization's problems. At the end of a particularly emotional memorial service at the Friends Meeting House, one of them refused to shake my hand. He literally turned his back on me and walked out. I had left Doug at home sick and was needing a lot of support myself. That kind of behavior wore me down, and as the situation at ECRA deteriorated I felt increasingly out of place. Lacking organizational cohesion, the board found its focus by turning on me, with members taking sides both for and against my continued presence. By saying I'd remain until the end of the year, I'd inadvertently made matters worse. Some wanted me to stay on beyond my announced resignation date in December, and others wanted me gone.

The battle lines were well and truly drawn and divided the organization even more deeply than before. The new chair and the vice president of the board got into a screaming match in the office. On top of that, the new office manager who'd been hired to replace Billy was a disaster. We were dealing with too many deaths, and too much grief and paying the price of structural disorganization. I felt helpless and decided to wait until a new board was elected before making any final decisions.

Eighty people attended the annual board meeting to elect new members in December, and an official parliamentarian was called in to run it according to Robert's Rules of Order. We met at St. John's Church in Bethesda. I've noticed that when you fill a room with angry Episcopalians, the temperature doesn't always go up, it goes down. It was an extremely painful meeting. Around nine o'clock, the parliamentarian tried to lighten the mood by observing, "Oh, look, it's starting to snow outside." As far as I could tell, it was colder inside.

A secret ballot was taken, and the slate of candidates that was against my staying on as chaplain won. I was out. They gave me two farewell gifts on the spot: a sweater from Gap and a prayer book. They had them all ready. The meeting ended around 10p.m. I couldn't get out of there fast enough. Now that a decision had been made, I was both sad and relieved.

It was a long night. Once I got outside the church, I found it was sleeting, not snowing, and the streets were slick with ice. There were pile-ups everywhere. I was driving carefully, but my car spun out of control at a roundabout and slid into a carload of Muslims. I couldn't believe how my day was going. I was wearing my clerical collar, and as we exchanged information, the Muslim driver told me they were on their way home from their mosque. I wanted to say, "I've just been with a bunch of Episcopalians—can I go home with you?"

I didn't make it home. I abandoned my car at the top of the hill near St. Patrick's church. It was so slippery that I slid down the hill and ended up spending the night at the home of Carlin Rankin and Dr. Fred Morgan, two friends who'd actively supported my ministry from the earliest years. Doug had driven to the board meeting separately and somehow made it home in one piece after emerging from a three-car pile-up at the bottom of that same hill while I was stuck at the top of the hill. Two members of the board also had difficulties getting home that night. One was in a multiple car crash, and another fell on the ice and broke her leg. What a night!

My Washington AIDS ministry had come to an end. In every organization with a board of directors, there's usually someone on the staff who represents its vision to the public and fulfills it in the community. Usually, that's an executive director. We didn't have such a position, so that left the job to me as chaplain. When I left, it seems I took the vision with me. The board never operated with full confidence again, and ECRA eventually merged with Samaritan Ministries. What had started with so much enthusiasm in 1987 soon was greatly reduced. By then, of course, much of our work was done. Advances in treatment protocols meant that death rates from AIDS would soon plummet.

CHAPTER FORTY-FOUR

FLORIDA

Doug and I spent Christmas with his parents in Fort Lauderdale that year. We had a good visit, and I decided to stay on in Florida when Doug returned home to Washington. I was unemployed after all, a man without a ministry. I had friends in Miami and Key West, so I headed south to Key West, one of my favorite drives.

I felt numb and depressed as I drove onto the seven-mile bridge leading to Key West, but the weather was superb. The sea was emerald green, and the sun sparkled off the waves. The windows were down, and the breeze was blowing through my hair. It seemed the perfect moment to begin screaming at the top of my lungs, and I did so all the way across the bridge. It was a cathartic release. Then I found a secluded beach and went skinny dipping in the ocean. It helped.

From Key West, I drove on to Miami and visited Roger Miller, a chaplain with an interfaith AIDS ministry based in Fort Lauderdale. I'd known Roger for years, and we often met at AIDS conferences. He was an openly gay minister in the United Church of Christ. When I let him know I'd left my AIDS ministry in Washington, he became excited. "I'm going to call Blount Grant and tell him they need to bring you down here as their chaplain," he said.

Blount Grant was a canon at the Episcopal cathedral in Miami. I knew some of the people at that cathedral, but I wasn't ready to take on a new job just yet. I was still recovering from my last year with ECRA and needed a little more time to step back and take stock.

I returned to Washington in February and, once home, soon

found myself feeling restless. I had no idea what to do next. I loved Washington and didn't want to leave. I had a lot of history there.

I was still unemployed on May 1st when I got a call asking me to come down to meet Canon Grant in Miami and talk about a new job. I had mixed feelings about doing so and asked for a few days to think about it. Several days later while attending a clergy conference in Virginia, I went canoeing along a stretch of calm river with one of my favorite people, Nancy Early. Nancy's a thoughtful and intuitive priest and friend, and I trusted her judgment. She paddled as I relaxed in the bow of the canoe. When I told her about the call from Miami, she lit up like a Roman candle. "Oh my God," she exclaimed. "Miami! It's the up-and-coming place to be!"

I immediately thought, "Oh hell, I'm going to Miami." Nancy had the gift of discernment, so if she thought it was a good idea, I'd at least go and talk to them. I flew down a couple of weeks later, and they convinced me to sign up as the new AIDS chaplain for Miami's Trinity Cathedral. It would be my job to start up a not-for-profit organization just as I'd done in Washington. I'd learned from my mistakes, though. I insisted that the board would be a small one, and I'd be the director. They agreed. Other than that, my work as a chaplain in Miami would proceed much along the same lines as in Washington.

Doug's health had continued to deteriorate, so I knew it would be good for him to be closer to his parents in Fort Lauderdale. He'd been in the hospital for five days in June with pneumocystis pneumonia, but now he was out. On July 1, we packed up and moved to Miami. Doug was feeble, so his parents came to Washington to drive him south. I followed with our two Welsh Corgis, Chauncy and Sophie.

I'd lived in the Washington area for twenty of the most intense years of my life. The last decade in particular had been a richly textured experience marked by suffering, death, grace, and love. In hindsight, it's clear that it was time for me to move on and embrace new opportunities.

Shortly before we left town, Jane Dixon, the Assistant Bishop of the Washington Diocese and a good friend, commented on my ministry and my work at the National Cathedral. "Jerry," she said, "you changed this cathedral and this diocese, and you changed them for the better." Jane had been a parishioner of mine at St. Patrick's when she was going through seminary, and I was gratified by her praise. I'd come to Washington as an outsider, and it was deeply affirming to be told I'd made a difference by someone who'd been there all along the way.

We had trouble finding a suitable place in Miami that would allow dogs, but finally settled on an apartment twenty miles from the cathedral. This was an inconvenience, but we were determined to make it work. We spent the summer of 1996 getting settled and acquainting ourselves with life in Miami.

Doug had been deeply depressed about his failing health and decided to break the spell by visiting good friends in Hawaii. Not long after his return, his doctors started him on a regimen of protease inhibitors, a new class of anti-viral drugs in the medical arsenal against AIDS. Protease inhibitors proved to be a game changer, the drug we'd all been hoping for. Replication of the HIV virus relies on the protease enzyme found in all healthy human bodies. Protease inhibitors interrupt that process so that the virus can no longer incapacitate the body's immune system.

The new treatment proved nothing short of a miracle for Doug. His health improved almost immediately. Doug underwent what was called The Lazarus Syndrome: He was brought back from the precipice of death. He never spent another night in the hospital due to AIDS. His fevers departed, and his energy returned.

By February of 1997, Doug was feeling so well that we took a ten-day trip to Italy. It was a restful getaway and gave no hint of what lay ahead. Shortly after we returned to Miami, Doug left for a weekend retreat for people with AIDS in Key West and came back with a stunning announcement: He'd decided to leave me.

He did his best to explain. He was about to turn 40. He was only 25 when first diagnosed with HIV. He stated that a part of him had died back then. Now he wanted the freedom to make up for those lost years and find himself.

I was devastated and angry. I'd come to terms with losing Ron to death, but divorce? It seemed unthinkable. It made no sense. We'd been together nearly six years, and I knew we loved each other. I couldn't comprehend his wanting to move out. We'd talked about buying a house and had even looked at real estate. Now I understood why he'd seemed distracted.

What saved me was therapy. I found Fred Fleischer, a Jungian therapist and Episcopal priest who'd also been a monk, and asked Doug if he'd go into couples' counseling with me. He agreed to do so if I agreed not to try to keep him in our relationship. "Actually," I said, "I'm worried I'm becoming your enemy."

It was a partial truth, but it was enough to persuade him to enter counseling together. That, as it turned out, was enough to set us both free. By our sixth session, I understood what Doug had been trying to tell me. I was able to affirm for myself his need to go forward on his own.

Something else that helped was a consultation with a psychic that a friend from Washington had given me as a farewell gift. I decided now was the time to use take advantage of the gift, albeit over the phone. The psychic, Claudia Handler, was low-key and insightful. "You swim in deep waters, and Doug swims in shallow waters," she told me. "If you don't let him go, ten years from now you'll still be obsessed with anger. But if you do release him, he'll remain part of your life forever."

She was right. I gave Doug my blessing, and he quickly lined up a new apartment in a bohemian gay neighborhood in Miami Beach. I continued therapy with Fred on my own for four more years until I left Miami in 2001. Doug and I have remained friends, and I've found in our friendship an occasional oasis for retreat and return over the years. He went on to get his license in nursing which is his profession to this day.

CHAPTER FORTY-FIVE

PAUL HAMPTON CROCKETT

My grieving the loss of Doug brought back memory of the death of Ron Bushnell and so many others. The month that Doug moved out of our apartment I met Paul Hampton Crockett at a party, a lawyer and author of *HIV Law*. Paul was deeply grieving the loss of his lover, Scott, just a year before. We were instantly bound together by our mutual grief. He was just beginning to write about his experience of love and loss. I cheered his writing on, and by that fall he had finished *Death Is An Imposter*. I read the book with assurance that we were profoundly connected with Scott's dead. When I finished reading it, I went swimming in the outdoor pool in the apartment complex where I now lived alone. While swimming in the pool and feeling exhilarated, my Ron came to me in a very playful way. He was laughing, and I began laughing so hard I had to stop swimming. I held onto the side of the pool and laughed and laughed. I was relieved there was no one else in the pool who might have thought I had gone crazy.

Paul and I designed a workshop entitled "Maintaining Healthy Relationships With Those We Love But See No Longer." We took the workshop on the road to AIDS conferences. At our first conference we had no idea if anyone would attend, but twenty-five people showed up. We discovered that people needed to share stories of their ongoing encounters with their loved ones who had died. Those stories were all very inspiring.

CHAPTER FORTY-SIX

THE EPISCOPAL AIDS MINISTRY

In the meantime, I set up our not-for-profit organization at the Miami cathedral as the Episcopal AIDS Ministry, Inc., and I was making progress in my new job.

Trinity Cathedral was built in the 1920s and is still a beautiful building. It was more progressive than many Episcopal churches in South Florida but not as liberal as the diocese in Washington had become, despite Miami's reputation as a place to let your hair down. I was the first openly gay priest to work there in an official capacity.

Miami was very different from Washington, D.C., a city where old money and political power walked hand in hand. It was a serious place. Miami was a city filled with light and color and lined by beautiful beaches. It was a place to have fun.

I began holding healing services and visiting the sick in local hospitals, much as I had in Washington. The social order was different, and fundraising for a not-for-profit was more difficult. However, there was a well-organized gay community that had honed its skills at fundraising for AIDS work, and a number of wealthy citizens gave generously to the cause. The chair of my board, Mario Leon, was well-connected and had been a very active board member of the Community Alliance Against AIDS. He was skilled, bright, and a delight to work with. His family had fled Cuba as a result of Castro's revolution.

During my first year in Miami, we staged a Halloween costume ball that we called Mask for AIDS. I decided to go in drag without telling anyone, just to see their reaction. It was time to resurrect "Connie." I hired a professional makeup artist, a young Catholic man who was so excited to be working on a priest that he spent three hours on my face. He did an outstanding job. I added the chiffon dress, the wig, earrings, and black gloves and headed off to the ball. I arrived about an hour late, and nobody recognized me. Mission accomplished!

"Connie of Arlington," now from Bal Harbour Village, was once again a hit. Connie had "arrived" in Miami, and I'd arrived along with her. My therapist suggested I imagine Connie in the pulpit when I preached because she put me in touch with a deeper, more creative part of myself. I've spared the church that sight, but Connie is often there with me in spirit. If I were elected Pope, I'd make every male do drag at least once in their lifetime—the full Monty—just so they could encounter the whole of their humanity more fully. It's intensely liberating.

In some ways, Connie's appearance at the fundraising ball was a celebration of survival. The enormous dark cloud under which so many of us had been living for so long was beginning to lift. Just as I'd been sustained by angels in human guise in Washington, angels appeared to help me in Miami, too.

Mario had been born in Cuba but came to the U.S. with his family after Castro took power. Another angel was the Reverend Marta Weeks, a multi-millionaire Episcopal priest, who gave generously of her time and money. Milton Ferrell, a prominent Miami lawyer and an Episcopal layman, inspired us with his passion and wise counsel as did Dr. Michael Stary, another angel who served on our board. Our board was a saving grace, especially since it had only eight members instead of the seventy-four we'd endured in Washington.

I couldn't have done it without the support and encouragement of our board chair, Mario Leon, and his partner Gilles. Mario's network of socially conscious friends organized two "Designing by Design" fundraisers that brought about an outpouring of creativity from sixty design teams who each constructed a fantastical setting for ten people to have dinner. These events raised money not only for the Episcopal AIDS ministry but several of the other AIDS organizations.

Throughout the epidemic a countless number of musicians, actors, writers, painters, and other creative types, were inspired to create works of art in the midst of all the death and tragedy. And creativity certainly abounded in Miami.

As the new protease inhibitor drugs brought an end to the dying, the focus of fundraising and political action shifted gradually from AIDS to civil rights for the broader lesbian, bisexual, gay, and transgendered community. In 1977, Florida's Dade County had passed an ordinance banning discrimination against homosexuals in employment, housing and public accommodation. It was the most progressive gay rights legislation in the country and provoked a strong backlash from conservative Christians. Anita Bryant, a well-known singer and spokesperson for the Florida Citrus Commission, jumped on the bandwagon and led an ultimately successful campaign to overturn the ordinance. Now, twenty years later, a grassroots organization called Save Dade sprang up to overturn the damage. I joined the group and actively participated in its work.

The Dean of Trinity Cathedral, Donald Krickbaum, and I held a press conference on the steps of the cathedral in support of proposed new legislation to repudiate the work of Bryant's campaign and restore the original anti-discrimination ordinance. A vote by the City Council was scheduled for the first week of December 1998 at the Dade County Courthouse. On the day of the vote, the atmosphere was tense inside the courthouse. Around 200 people were in the courtroom as hundreds more waited outside. The council heard testimony from both sides, and then the vote was taken. The council was evenly divided with only one member on the fence, an African American, so suspense ran high. In the end, he moved over to our side of the fence, and the measure to ban discrimination on the basis of sexual orientation passed by one vote. It was a deeply satisfying moment.

In the fall of that year, Matthew Shepard was murdered in Laramie, Wyoming, and his brutal death served as a flashpoint for political action against hate crimes throughout the country. Gay communities across America rallied in support of measures to strengthen protections for gay people against violent crime. To highlight the issues, we held an interfaith service for Matthew at Temple Sinai in Miami and a large, well-attended candlelight memorial service outside The Score, a gay dance bar in Miami Beach. Both events garnered significant media coverage for our cause.

CHAPTER FORTY-SEVEN

NASSAU

By the spring of 2000, my work as an AIDS chaplain in Miami was less hectic. Although I continued to visit people with AIDS in hospitals, there were far fewer funerals, and the epidemic had mercifully lost its momentum. When I was invited to be on a radio program in Nassau, capital of the Bahamas, I had no hesitation in agreeing to do so. The ministry could spare me for a couple of days.

Battles over gay rights were raging throughout the Caribbean. The biggest issue was whether individual islands would allow gay cruise ships to dock at their ports. The cruise lines were all for it. It was big business for them, but ignorance and prejudice among island political and religious leaders led them to oppose letting the ships in. In Nassau, Anglican Archbishop Drexel Gomez led a group of interfaith ministers who claimed that gay tourists would ruin the Bahamas' reputation as a romantic honeymoon spot because "the homosexuals will seduce the newly-wed husbands away from their brides." Who can reason against that sort of logic?

A Bahamian radio personality wanted to host a debate on the issue that included a pro-gay member of the local clergy, but he couldn't find one who was willing to speak publicly. My therapist, Fred, heard they were looking. He owned a house in Nassau and put the radio station in touch with me after securing my permission. They flew me over to debate a Baptist minister who'd agreed to represent the opposing point of view.

The radio show was an hour-long live transmission, and it aired on a Sunday evening. Supposedly, the Baptist minister was only moderately anti-gay, and so he seemed at the beginning.

That impression collapsed when I said that one of the channels I'd found to The Divine was through my love for my lover. The Baptist lost it on the spot. He became over-the-top hysterical in his furious denunciations. I was thrilled. The show ran twenty minutes overtime and generated a flood of call-ins by listeners. My host took me to a gay bar after the show, and it became apparent I had a fan club in Nassau. The warrior in me was fighting on a new frontier.

In September of 2001, I was invited back to take part in Nassau's first Gay Pride Festival. Homophobia was still the order of the day, so it would take place behind closed doors and not in the streets. I took Tommie Lee Watkins, a gay African American minister, with me. In total, about fifty people participated. It was only a four-day visit, but we made the most of it. We led an interfaith service in a lesbian bar, and "Connie" put in an appearance at a private party on an exotic tropical night.

As the party wound down, an acquaintance to one of the participants—also in drag—warned me not to go back to the hotel dressed as Connie. It was too dangerous; I'd likely be attacked. His warning reminded me that the same thing could happen in many parts of the world. Living in large, relatively progressive cities for over thirty-five years had dulled my awareness. AIDS wasn't the only threat to homosexuals in much of the world.

CHAPTER FORTY-EIGHT

END OF AN ERA

Back in Miami, the emphasis of our ministry was changing from AIDS to drug abuse. Deaths from AIDS had declined significantly since the arrival of protease inhibitors, but many had turned to using crystal meth, a highly addictive drug that affects the central nervous system. OxyContin had also begun to be over-subscribed as a pain medication.

In 2000, I had convinced my board to take over a small HIV medical outreach clinic that was serving Miami's large Haitian community. The doctor who'd set up the clinic was moving to another city, and I saw this as an opportunity to broaden our outreach. Not everyone on the board supported the decision, and two of them resigned in protest. We nevertheless pushed forward and hired one of our board members to direct the new program.

Within three months, we discovered we were in way over our heads financially. We found that some of our patients were using the clinic primarily to gain access to pain medications, mostly OxyContin, which they'd then sell on the streets. Once we faced the enormity of the challenges facing the clinic, we realized we weren't up to the task. We didn't have the expertise to operate a medical facility under these circumstances.

After we closed the clinic, the former board member we'd appointed to direct its operations stormed the bishop's office and insisted he be reinstated. I had to eat humble pie and admit my idea had failed. My idealism has been both a blessing and a curse, but I've never been able to shake it. In this case, it had led us in the wrong direction.

Even though AIDS was becoming a manageable chronic condition, our weekly healing services at the cathedral continued to draw men and women, gay and straight, from a wide social and racial demographic. We invited a cross section of spiritual leaders from rabbis, Catholic sisters, and Pentecostal preachers to speak. We often had twenty or more congregants at any given service. We also carried on with our retreats for people with AIDS, which we held at Bon Secours, a center run by Catholic nuns.

Our retreats were as popular in Miami as they had been in Washington. On the last evening of the retreats, the staff served a fancy dinner, and I would get dressed up in drag as my alter-ego, "Connie from Bal Harbour," and play hostess. Sister Elizabeth, our contact person at the Bon Secours center, was an open-hearted delight and always supportive of our work. But not everyone liked Connie. After Sister Elizabeth was transferred to another facility just before our last retreat, Connie was banned. I was told that "the help" in the kitchen were disturbed by Connie's presence. Not the nuns, the help. Right. We staged our last retreat in 2001 and Connie, indeed, was disinvited.

Our last retreat was also one of the most memorable. In my small discussion group were a young gay white man with AIDS who'd been rejected by his Roman Catholic family and a middle-aged heterosexual African American man who was in recovery from drug addiction. The older man shared with the group that his 18-year-old daughter had been killed in a car accident a year before. He'd spent all his money on drugs and couldn't even buy flowers for her funeral. He'd recently learned that his 20-year-old son was gay. He was at a loss, because he didn't know how to relate to his son and was afraid he was going to lose him, too.

The young gay man gently advised the older man how to approach his son. The two of them, opposites in many ways, formed a close bond that weekend. The father had never visited his daughter's grave, so they agreed that after the retreat they would visit it together.

By 2001, I'd participated in forty AIDS retreats, and all of them had been spiritually grounding and uplifting. They had constituted a "temenos," a sacred safe space where people could be themselves authentically and without fear, a place apart from a world in which they could be anything but. They had given immeasurable comfort to people with AIDS and those of us who cared for them.

Although my workload was lighter now that people were surviving AIDS, my soul was weary. Suffering and death and the politics of engaging them had grown burdensome. I was 59 years old, and I felt like I'd been in the vanguard of the church's AIDS ministry for an eternity. It was time again for a change.

CHAPTER FORTY-NINE

LEAVING FLORIDA

Friends in South Africa invited me to participate in a Pan-African clergy conference on AIDS scheduled for the summer of 2001. Although they offered to pay my way, I had mixed feelings about attending. I'd been there six years earlier and wanted to see Africa again, but the climate for gay Christians in Africa was discouraging. Most Anglican bishops in Africa were biased against homosexuals, and many remain so to this day. I was tired of doing battle with homophobic Christians, and that's what this conference would likely be all about. As the date drew near, my friends sent word that they hadn't been able to raise the money to fly me over after all. I was greatly relieved by this news and delighted to contemplate a block of suddenly available free time.

Albert Ogle was a gay priest in the Diocese of Los Angeles and, like me, had been an AIDS warrior. He'd worked at the L.A. Gay and Lesbian Center and was one of the founders of the Pasadena AIDS Coalition. In the early 1980s, he'd been hired by a large Episcopal church on the West Coast and then fired within 24 hours when the vestry found out he was gay. Albert and I had worked together on the issue of AIDS since 1988. I'd visited him in Laguna Beach, California in the past, and now he invited me to spend a couple of weeks with him in August.

The timing was perfect. The humidity in Miami is awful that time of year, and Laguna Beach was a happy alternative. Albert and I enjoyed hanging out together at the gay beach in Laguna. I sometimes think Albert scatters fairy dust on people. I suspect he's an Irish witch. Our conversations during that visit helped me see myself with a clarity that had been obscured by the intensity of the work I'd done for so many years. I'd become a burnout case, and

Albert helped me realize I needed to make some changes.

During my visit with Albert, I arranged to have lunch with another old friend from my AIDS work, Thad Bennett, who was working as the staff deployment officer for the Diocese of Los Angeles. I gently broached the subject of vacancies in Los Angeles. He mentioned a few possibilities, and that Sunday, I drove to Hollywood to attend a service at St. Thomas Church. This parish had a large outreach to the gay community, and it was looking for a new rector.

I wanted to observe the parish and its congregation unobtrusively, so I left my clerical collar at home. As I sat in the back pew that morning, it dawned on me that it was almost fifteen years to the day since that fateful birthday dinner for Terry when we'd learned my friend Logan had AIDS and I'd been eliminated from the list of applicants to become rector of St. Margaret's Church. So much had changed for the better in the intervening years. AIDS was no longer a death sentence, and the church was far more open to its gay and lesbian members, both clerical and lay. It wasn't beyond the realm of possibility that I could apply to become rector of this church and actually be accepted. Just the thought of it brought me to tears. In that moment, I knew I would resign from my ministry in Miami and explore new possibilities in California. A heavy burden had lifted.

When I returned to Miami and told the board of my decision, they didn't offer any opposition; they understood. I gave them my resignation effective at the end of November 2001. Before I left, however, there would be one final hurrah.

In 1981, Public Radio's Diane Rehm had been on the St. Patrick's vestry that voted me in as the assistant rector. She'd moderated our first interfaith AIDS conference in 1987, and she'd had me on her talk show several times over the years. She'd been a strong advocate for my work and generous with air time as her show became increasingly popular. By the time I moved to Florida, she was a renowned National Public Radio celebrity. We reconnected when she came to Miami for a book signing in 1998, and I got to show her around town.

By 2001, word had gotten around that I knew Diane. A local university asked if I would invite her to come down from Washington to speak at their fundraising luncheon. The local public radio station also wanted to host a fundraising breakfast with her as the speaker. These dates were set for October long before I knew I would be leaving Miami. Diane accepted the two invitations, and it took several months to coordinate these events to coincide with a single visit on her part.

On September 11, two weeks before Diane's scheduled visit, terrorists attacked New York's World Trade Center and the Pentagon in Washington, D.C. Flights across the country were disrupted, and there was some confusion about the available flights Diane could take to get to Miami. Someone at our end dropped the ball, and Diane canceled her visit. I was dismayed by the prospect of Diane's not attending my farewell event. I thought the world of her and had looked forward to seeing her again. The university and radio fundraisers were beside themselves. Also, her husband John did not want her to get on a plane.

I called Diane and, with help from someone at the university, we sorted things out. Diane arrived to great fanfare, and I escorted her to the university luncheon where about fifty major donors were seated. In the middle of her speech, she said, "I want you all to know that you need to thank Father Anderson, who is sitting in the back of the room, because he is the reason I'm here." I was pleased by her support and wished I'd met these donors when I first arrived in Miami. It would have made my own fundraising efforts a cakewalk by comparison.

That night, Diane spoke at my farewell service at Trinity Cathedral. The bishop was presiding, and the dean was there along with fifty or so other friends and colleagues. Diane offered lovely tribute in which she called my work "courageous" and shared her own perceptions of my ministry all the way back to those early years at St. Patrick's. I cried all the way through it.

The next morning, I slipped through the back door at the radio station's fundraising breakfast just as Diane began her speech to the several hundred people gathered for the event. As soon as I entered the room, she pointed at me and said, "There! Father Anderson just arrived. You can thank him. He's the one responsible for my being here after I'd canceled."

Diane had been there at the beginning of my AIDS ministry in Washington, and she was there at the end in Miami. Her appearance at my farewell service was a treasured gift. I and so many others are forever in her debt. She, too, was an angel who helped carry me through.

CHAPTER FIFTY

California Here I Come

I encountered many signs and portents as I prepared to leave for California, and they all reassured me I was heading in the right direction. I was told by one woman that I emitted a "golden glow" whenever I spoke of my plans to move out west. I hit the road in November of 2001 and stayed with various friends along the way. I stopped in San Antonio, Texas and had a meal with Brother Coote, the former president of my old Bible college. Over dinner, Brother Coote, who was now 81 years old, told me that his son, Tim, had died of AIDS. I'd known Tim when he was just a kid, and it was obvious even then that he was gay. I finally told Brother Coote that I was gay and then asked if Tim had been gay. "Not when he died!" he replied. He reported they had sent him to Oral Roberts University and they "gave him" a gay roommate, as if that had been what had turned him gay.

It seems that Tim, on his death bed, had been browbeaten into repenting and recanting his homosexuality. Brother Coote wondered aloud if he had been neglectful of his duties as a father and was somehow responsible that Tim had been gay.

"Brother Coote," I said, "I can tell you from personal experience that you could have taken Tim hunting and fishing every day of his boyhood, and it would have made no difference." He had no response.

For old times' sake, I attended a worship service at the Bible college chapel the next morning, and it was miserable experience. The atmosphere was as drab and depressing as it had been 40 years earlier. "Thank God I didn't get stuck here," I thought to myself. "Thank God I got out."

I loved driving across the country and was upbeat and optimistic almost the entire way. I did, however, suffer a brief relapse when I reached Yuma, Arizona. While waiting for my lunch in a modest mall restaurant, I was unexpectedly besieged by anxiety and doubts. "What in the hell are you doing?" I thought to myself. "You don't have a job, and you have left everything behind. And AIDS ministry is the only work you've known for the past fifteen years, so now what?" These were depressing thoughts, so I tried to call my sister and got no answer. I called a couple of close friends and couldn't get through to them, either. Perhaps a bit of shopping would help?

As I wandered through the mall after my lunch, I noticed some beautiful landscape paintings in a small gallery window and walked in for a closer look. The paintings were lovely in themselves and imbued with an elusive spiritual quality. Noticing my interest, the owner of the gallery asked if I'd like to meet the painter. "He's right over there," she pointed.

I turned around to see a kindly looking man in his fifties with long gray hair in a ponytail talking to a friend. I walked over and introduced myself. He was pleased that I'd responded to the spiritual quality of his work and asked what I did for a living. When I told him I was an Episcopal priest, he responded that he, too, was a minister—a charismatic Pentecostal minister, no less.

When it came time for me to leave, he asked if he could say a prayer for me before I departed. "Of course," I replied. Then and there, in the middle of the art gallery, he prayed a beautiful prayer over me, and the owner and his friend joined in. As they prayed, all the worry and doubt I'd felt just a short time before vanished into the light of their love.

I thanked them, and the artist-minister accompanied me out to the parking lot. From there he led me in his car out of Yuma all the way to the interstate where he waved me across the border into California, my new home. I couldn't have scripted my arrival any better if I'd tried.

Epilogue

The years since I arrived in Southern California in the fall of 2001 have been some of the best of my life. Two weeks after arriving, I met Shane Bruce and hired him to be my physical fitness trainer in Laguna Beach. Little did I know how this would impact my life. He had moved to California five years prior from New York City to care for his mother who was dying of cancer. After her death, he then cared for his Godfather, an Episcopal priest who also died of cancer. Shane introduced me to his social circle who took me in and made me feel at home.

Within a couple months of arriving, I was appointed the part-time Pastoral Interim Priest at St. Paul's Church in Pomona. This was to last thirteen months and gave me the challenge of helping the congregation make the transition after the retirement of its rector of twenty-nine years. Half-time work meant I had lots of time to watch sunsets over the Pacific Ocean and grieve the loss of so much back east.

In May of 2003, Bishop Jon Bruno of the Diocese of Los Angeles appointed me the director of Pastoral Care at Good Samaritan Hospital in downtown L.A., which had been founded by the Episcopal Church in 1885. By this time, my relationship with Shane had taken on a primary importance in my life. We decided to move to L.A. together. Shane had wanted for a long time to get a Master's degree in psychology. He enrolled in the Pacifica Graduate Institute, graduated three years later, and was then licensed by the State to become a therapist.

Meanwhile, at the hospital I was given the task of rebuilding the Department of Pastoral Care. With assistance from the Bishop and key board members, we were able to raise enough funding to add a Spanish-speaking Catholic chaplain, and then to hire the Reverend Ronald David MD to establish a clinical pastoral training program for seminarians and clergy. We also restored the iconic All Souls Chapel which had been built in 1926, along with its Skinner pipe organ.

AIDS did not disappear from my life entirely as several of my friends became long-term survivors—the protease inhibitor protocols that were introduced in the mid 90s reduced the virus in their blood streams to undetectable levels. It has been a great joy to witness them return to the fullness of health and to life's adventure. We would, from time to time, have a patient in the hospital who had not been properly screened for the HIV virus who became sick with AIDS.

In 2007, Shane and I co-produced a musical stage production he wrote entitled, "Being Poz' The Musical!" The play depicts a love story between two young men, one of whom is HIV positive while the other is HIV negative. We raised two productions with two different directors and casts. It was well received, and it portrayed the many complexities that face those living with HIV/AIDS. Bishop Bruno underwrote the cost of one production, which enabled us to contribute 100 percent of the sold-out box office proceeds to a Los Angeles-based HIV/AIDS service facility.

I retired from Good Samaritan Hospital at age 74 in 2016. We then moved to a small seaside town near Santa Barbara, where I am a priest-associate at All Saints By The Sea in Montecito. Shane has a full-time practice as an ADHD Depth and Productivity Coach, and he continues to write and perform his music.

END